Robert Louis Stevenson – Bright Ring of Words

COMPILED & EDITED BY
ALANNA KNIGHT &
ELIZABETH STUART WARFEL

BALNAIN

published in 1994 by
Balnain Books
Druim House
Lochloy Road
Nairn IV12 5LF
Scotland

Printed and bound by The Cromwell Press, Melksham

Cataloguing in Publication Data:
A catalogue record for this book is available from the British Library

ISBN 1 872557 32 5

ACKNOWLEDGEMENTS

Georgetown University. RLS Restorations & Preservations Foundation (James Michener, Stevenson House, Monterey & State of California *'Notes from His Mother's Diary'*) Scribners Sons Ltd and Chatto & Windus (excerpts from *'An Intimate Portrait of RLS'* (1924) T B Osbourne Schieferle, executrix of her grandfather Lloyd Osbourne's estate. Silverado Museum,St Helena, California (photographs of Lloyd Osbourne) Finally, we pay tribute to all Stevensonian experts and enthusiasts not in this volume for one reason or another, but nevertheless deserving of a space (many with a fine tale to tell!), especially Robin Hill, former Assistant Curator of Museums, Edinburgh, for his never-ending help to us all; the late Ellen Shaffer of the Silverado Museum, Silverado; Alistair Ferguson, secretary of the Robert Louis Stevenson Club, Edinburgh for his on-going help and services; and Lady Dunpark, formerly of 17 Heriot Row, Edinburgh whose door was always open and welcoming.

Our special thanks to all the contributors for so generously donating their fees to the following charities:

The Robert Louis Stevenson Club Fund for the relief of respiratory diseases in Children; Sick Kids Hospital, Edinburgh; The Ayrshire Aids Hospice.

CONTENTS

IV. THE WANDERER ('LOUIS')

V. THE EXILE ('TUSITALA')

DEDICATION

To Dick (CR) Warfel
Rick and Marion Warfel
Lesley and David Slifkin
and in loving memory of
their sister Elise Warfel Ryan

FOREWORD

The contributors came in all shapes, sizes and ages, from all places, but the word that recurred throughout each of the varied experiences with Stevenson is 'friendship'. 'A genius for friendship', 'scattered friendships': the catalyst which unites contributors from many different walks of life, from Scotland to Samoa, from Portobello to Pasadena, from Ayr to Australia, from the Napa Valley to New Zealand.

In common with the best of Stevenson's ideas, our concept of a 'Centennial Celebration' evolved atmospherically one chilly November night by a cheery fire in a converted fisherman's cottage in East Lothian. We were discussing a possible use for the original sheet music of 'Aberlady Links' composed by Stevenson and in his own hand found in the vaults of the Stevenson House in Monterey, California. Conversation drifted to how many new friends Stevenson had introduced into our lives.

'Wouldn't it be great,' said Elizabeth, 'if we could spread the word, get together all those other people out there, everywhere — whose lives have been changed and influenced by RLS as ours have been.'

To paraphrase Stevenson: The next thing we knew, we had some paper before us and were writing out a list of names. How often had we done so and the thing gone no farther! But there seemed elements of success about this enterprise.

We approached contributors tentatively. Their response was overwhelming with replies immediate, enthusiastic and delighted.Only a small few fell by the wayside due to temporary indisposition, long-term illness or pressure of academic work.

Correspondence grew into several files including tantalising appetisers like Graham Greene's letter dated 12th November 1985 to Sir James Marjoribanks, then Chairman of the RLS Club Appeals Committee:

> '...I still read with pleasure *Weir of Hermiston*, *Dr Jekyll and Mr Hyde* and *The Master of Ballantrae*. I am sure I would enjoy too *Treasure Island* which I haven't read for some

years. I think it was Stevenson's method of describing action without adjectives or adverbs which taught me a good deal. The reader may think that action in a novel is easier than dialogue, but the contrary is true, and so many writers get their action with the help of adjectives. Even the most violent action in *Treasure Island* is conveyed as I remember without the use of adjectives.'

There was also a timely missive in a personal letter from James Michener dated 4 February 1991 to Jim Winegar, President of the RLS Preservation Restoration Foundation in Samoa, who sent it on to us for possible inclusion in our book:

'... I certainly approve of your efforts to memorialize RLS properly, for when I compare him and Gauguin and Maugham — all of whom I've been reflecting upon recently — it seems to me that RLS conducted himself more humanely than any of the others. So push ahead.'

One wonders what else Michener could have said...?

Fay Ala'ilma's contribution came in the old Samoan fashion of the 'Talking Man' or Orator, speaking for his or, in this case, her Chief on important occasions. That Tusitala's 'Celebration' merits such consideration was one of the high points in the planning stages of this book and it is appropriate that this evocative account of her people should be our last 'living' contribution in a list ranging from a privileged childhood at Colinton Manse, a boyhood in Edinburgh of the 1920s (with a father-son relationship tortuous as Stevenson's own), to a literary detective story at the Bridge of Allan. From geographically and spiritually different walks of life they came; professors and dancers, actors and biographers, editors and musicians, dedicated Stevensonians and Samoans. And linking them together Maggie Stevenson's diary and Lloyd Osbourne's 'Intimate Portrait,' reprinted here for the first time in 70 years.

The common denominator shining like gold through many and varied experiences is that Stevenson was a man for all times, all seasons and all peoples. The genius of Stevenson lay in who and what he was, the amazement of personal identification and enrichment that discovery had brought.

To quote Trevor Royle: 'Not for the first time Stevenson's ideas were striking exactly the right kind of note for a later day and age...' And one fact emerges clear and outstanding: how well his revolutionary concepts would have fitted into the world of the 1990s.

The final editing was completed more than a year later in

Scotland where it had all begun: '... *so our road came in the end to lie very near due north: the old kirk of Aberlady for a landmark on the left; on the right the top of Berwick Law.*' So wrote Stevenson in Catriona.

Favourite contributions? Well, yes, of course, but like a doting parent who loves all her children equally there is still the vital spark that sets them apart: individual style, original turn of phrase or mystical interpretation of experience. Like the many facets of Stevenson himself there is something for everyone and that is the continuing magic of it all.

Alanna Knight and Elizabeth Stuart Warfel
Aberlady, February 1993

7 October 1993

I am delighted and honoured to have been asked to make this contribution, small though it is, to this publication in honour of Robert Louis Stevenson who lived the last five years of his life in Samoa a century ago.

The Samoans were thrilled to have a world-renowned author living amongst them and they proudly named him Tusitala — Writer of Stories. Tusitala's fame assured him the recognition and respect of his new neighbours; however, it was his humility which earned him a special place in the hearts of the Samoans.

From the begining, Tusitala displayed a keen interest in the people of Samoa and the turbulent affairs of the country. He worked hard at trying to understand the causes of the upheaval in Samoa at the time, and he also actively involved himself in efforts to bring about peace and order. His active participation was not always welcomed particularly by the representatives of the three powers — Germany, the United States, and Great Britain — who had signed the Berlin treaty in 1889 bringing Samoa under their tripartite control; they regarded Tusitala as an Adventurer who was interfering in political matters which were not his concern.

The Samoans saw Tusitala in a different light. They had quickly come to recognise in him a nobility of spirit which was reflected in all his dealings with them. He respected their faa-Samoa — the Samoan way of life — and he was sensitive to its requirements although he clearly did not understand many of its elements. They found him to be a man of great warmth and humour, sharp intelligence and unbounded creativity; he was attentive and perceptive, and keenly interested in everything that went on around him. The Samoans had *no doubts that Tusitala had a genuine and sincere concern for their welfare and the well-being of their country. They gave him their trust and their love.*

When Tusitala died, the Samoans cleaved a path through the thick rain forest on the steep side of Mount Vaea next to his home, and carried him in his coffin to his final resting place on the summit. They called the path the 'Road of the Loving Hearts' which indicated the difficulty of their task and their love for Tusitala.

We remember Tusitala as a good man and his memory will live on in the hearts of the people of Samoa. His contribution to world literature was a major one, and it is fitting that the world community should join in this tribute to his life of service and creativity.

Soifua.

(Toilau Eti Alesana)
PRIME MINISTER

Aberlady Links — written by RLS

PART I

THE CHILD
'SMOUT'

SIR JAMES MARJORIBANKS

VICE CONSUL IN NEW YORK · FOREIGN OFFICE · APPOINTMENTS INCLUDE ASSISTANT UNDER SECRETARY OF STATE · DIRECTOR OF THE DISTILLERS CO. · CHAIRMAN FOR SCOTLAND IN EUROPE

SERVED WITH H M EMBASSY, PEKING · MA (HONS) EDINBURGH · CONSULATE GENERAL IN HANKOW & MARSEILLES & CONSUL IN JACKSONVILLE

MARVELLOUS PLACES THOUGH HANDY TO HOME

MARVELLOUS PLACES THOUGH HANDY TO HOME

SIR JAMES MARJORIBANKS

I own I like definite form in what my eyes are to rest upon; and if landscapes were sold, like the sheets of characters of my childhood, one penny plain and twopence coloured, I should go the length of twopence every day of my life.

TRAVELS WITH A DONKEY

Until he was ten years old Robert Louis Stevenson spent his summer holidays at Colinton Manse where lived his maternal grandfather Dr Lewis Balfour. The Manse lies a mere four miles from the centre of Edinburgh but in its silvan setting forms a complete contrast to the city landscape. Its beautiful garden on a peninsula in the Water of Leith was the inspiration for several of the poems in his *Child's Garden of Verses*, a book he worked on intermittently for a number of years often as a relaxation from more serious craftsmanship.

In his essay *Memories and Portraits* he talks of it lovingly as a: 'place in that time like no other; the garden cut into provinces by a great hedge of beech, and overlooked by the church and the terrace of the churchyard, where the tombstones were thick, and after nightfall 'spunkies' might be seen to dance, at least by children: flower pots lying warm in sunshine; laurels and the great yew making elsewhere a pleasing horror of shade; the smell of water rising from all round, with an added tang of paper mills; the sound of water everywhere and the sound of mills, the wheel and the dam singing their alternate strain; the birds on every bush and from every corner of the overhanging woods pealing out their notes until the air throbbed with them; and in the midst of this, the manse!'

My father was one of Dr Balfour's successors as Minister of Colinton and occupied the pulpit from 1910 to 1934. I was born in 1911 closely followed by a little sister. To have entered life within the dear old walls of Colinton Manse was a privilege indeed and in my first twenty-four years I most happily shared Stevenson's deep regard for that: 'well beloved house, its image fondly dwelt on by many travellers.'

I can never think of any house that bequeaths more of its graciousness and innate homeliness to its surroundings than this old grey mansion by the riverside, with woods rising to the sky all round it and yet with its lawns and flowerbeds always penetrable by whatever sunshine was going. The best rooms in the house on the first floor had been allocated by my parents to the children as 'nursery' and 'night nursery'. My elder brother Will and I slept in the nursery, a spacious chamber with a southern bow window and two other windows looking up to the Church which stood beside the Manse at a slightly higher elevation.

> *The great day nursery, best of all,*
> *With pictures pasted on the wall*
> *And leaves upon the blind*
> *A pleasant room wherein to wake*
> *And hear the leafy garden shake*
> *And rustle in the wind ...*

The sound of the river is everywhere present and as Stevenson says its sound has never left the ears of those who were brought up in the Manse. The Water of Leith was one of the many rivers that made music in his memory and his favourite viewpoint was, 'at a certain water-door, embowered in shrubbery. The river is there dammed back for the service of the flour mill just below, so that it lies deep and darkling, and the sand slopes into brown obscurity with a glint of gold...'

> *The river on from mill to mill,*
> *Flows past our childhood's garden still:*
> *'But ah! we children never more*
> *Shall watch it from the water-door!'*

The manse garden at night assumed a different aspect when night approached.

> *All round the house is the jet-black night;*
> *It stares through the window-pane;*
> *It crawls in the corners, hiding from the light,*
> *And moves with the moving flame.*
>
> *Now my little heart goes a-beating like a drum,*
> *With the breath of the Bogie in my hair;*
> *And all round the candle the crooked shadows come*
> *And go marching along up the stair.*
>
> *The shadow of the balusters, the shadow of the lamp,*
> *The shadow of the child that goes to bed,*
> *All the wicked shadows coming tramp, tramp, tramp,*
> *With the black night overhead.'*

As I went up to bed, holding my candle, I used to feel myself the principal actor in this shadow march and enjoyed with Robert Louis the satisfaction of coming, 'from out the cold and gloom into my warm and cheerful room.'

Stevenson was very sensitive to the rather eerie proximity of the churchyard next to the Manse. The scene on a foggy November night can indeed be a bit creepy. The churchyard did not escape the attentions of the body-snatchers, one of its features being a large iron 'mort safe' which used to be placed over the coffin after burial to discourage predators.

The path under the churchyard retaining wall was named 'the Witches Walk' and led to the giant yew tree, at least three hundred years old whose branches form something of an amphitheatre where we could play impervious to the elements for hours on end. How we did like to go up in that swing which still hangs from one of the inner branches. 'Beneath the yew, it still is there, our phantom voices haunt the air as we were still at play. And I can hear them call and say: How far is it to Babylon?'

In Stevenson's day, the land to the south of the Manse was occupied by a paper mill whose humming of thunder inspired one of the most evocative of his poems.

> *Over the borders, a sin without pardon,*
> *Breaking the branches and crawling below,*
> *Out through the breach in the wall of the garden,*
> *Down by the banks of the river, we go.*
>
> *Here is the mill with the humming of thunder,*
> *Here is the weir with the wonder of foam,*
> *Here is the sluice with the race running under*
> *Marvellous places, though handy to home!*

My brothers and I used to play cricket on the lawn in front of the house and often the cricket ball would go through that breach in the wall of the garden and so to retrieve it down by the banks of the river we went. You were always 'out' if you hit the ball into the Water of Leith (h.i.r) You were also 'out', I hasten to say, if you hit the ball into the churchyard (h.i.c.)

Another of our ploys was to make a ladder up the back of the yew tree trunk by means of wooden spars nailed into the soft bark which enabled us to scale its height of some sixty feet in almost as many seconds. And what a joy to stand in the topmost branches with the smell of the yew berries and the sense of achievement at being 'on top of the world.' There were other great trees too, a deodar at the far end of the lawn screening the garden from the churchyard (its seed had been sent back from India in a letter by a former son of the Manse) and a great elm which hung over the river and our 'riverside walk' created by my father and my eldest brother George on their billhooking Saturdays, which led right along the garden perimeter. I recall the ceremonial opening of the riverside walk when little sister Anne was pushed round it in her go-cart having previously snipped an inaugural ribbon.

My father in his outward appearance, may have borne some affinity to Stevenson's grandfather. He was very tall and of a rather austere aspect but his character was in complete contrast to the picture Stevenson paints of Dr Lewis Balfour, a "somewhat awful figure" who would not allow his grandson "a barley sugar kiss" because he had not, as grandfather had, been first dosed with Gregory's Powder. Indeed, my father, on the other hand, had a quite extraordinarily alarming sense of humour. My mother used to keep a flock of hens under the shadow of the churchyard and we used to tease her about a White Leghorn cock of which she was very proud. Like the cock in the Bible this bird had the habit of crowing frequently and used to put my father off during his sermon. He was terrified lest he should get the giggles in the pulpit. My eldest brother and I were therefore given the task on a Sunday morning of catching the cock and locking it up in the stable. The hens are no more and from the stable, now transformed into a modern Sunday school, come sounds perhaps more pleasing to the ear than those of the poultry yard.

In my memories of happy childhood days at Colinton, I am conscious of the fact that the whole scene, the garden, the river, the mill, the old grey manse was always illumined by Robet Louis's genius and his extraordinary talent for investing simple scene and objects with the magic light of childhood. The poems in the *Child's Garden of Verses* are not wholly fanciful; the magic has always a homely counterpart:

marvellous places though handy to home
a thousand miles we galloped fast
at last we drew rein... in time for tea.

The combination of dramatic fancy with sober description is a feature I have always noticed and prized in Stevenson's essays. His power as a novelist seems to spring from the intensity of his dramatic imagination. But he was nevertheless capable of keeping his fancy in check and never allowed it to damage the main purpose of his writing. His childhood days at Colinton Manse were clearly most important in his later life.

At an early and extremely impressionable age he was immersed in and deeply impressed by the delights and drama of the Colinton household. If, as he believed, environment is as important as friendship in moulding a man's mind, then the manse's romantic setting must have exercised a profound influence on Robert Louis's development as an author. In his case the child is clearly father of the man.

I grew up closely in sympathy with Stevenson's descriptions of the various garden subjects. The river, the yew, the laurels still retain their magic whenever I have the chance to visit the Manse. If I were asked what influence these features held for me in my subsequent career, I think I would say that the essential message of the *Child's Garden* is a homely one, of a child happily settled in a cheerful environment, where his imagination could be given full rein. To have shared in this picture was an incalculable bonus. It gave one confidence in the basic stability of one's origins. And this is a strong foundation amid the trials and complexities of later life.

Although I said I was closely in sympathy with Stevenson's Colinton impressions, there was one phrase in relation to the Manse which I did not appreciate: 'The Old Manse has changed today; it wears an altered face and shields a stranger race.'

I did not consider myself part of a stranger race. It was my lawn, my yew tree, my river just as much as RLS's. But in this thought lies perhaps the key to the garden's charm; it has been in a very personal way the perfect garden for a long succession of children. *The Child's Garden of Verses* is known of course to children the world over. Most of the illustrations in the countless editions adorning nursery shelves bear little resemblance to any features in the Colinton landscape. But that is perhaps as it should be. For it is only right and proper that children reading the book should in their mind's eye make Stevenson's garden their own.

DAVID ANGUS

POET, LECTURER, JOURNALIST · AUTHORITY ON THE EARLIER LIFE OF R.L.S · 2 BOOKS: A GUIDE TO THE EDINBUGH WAX MUSEUM AND ROSES & THORNS (ANTHOLOGY VERSE)

BORN: BRORA IN 1925 · EDUCATION: IN HIGHLANDS & LANARK & EDINBURGH UNIVERSITY MA (HONS) · SERVED IN THE ROYAL NAVY. TAUGHT FOR SOME 20 YEARS

TRAVELLING HOPEFULLY

TRAVELLING HOPEFULLY
DAVID ANGUS

The day had been warm; H— and I had played together
charmingly all day in a sandy wilderness across the
road; then came evening with a great flash of colour
and a heavenly sweetness in the air. Somehow my play-
mate had vanished or is out of the story, as the sagas
say, but I was sent into the village on an errand; and,
taking a book of fairy tales, went down alone through
fir-wood, reading while I walked. How often since then
it has befallen me to be happy so; but that was the first
time; the shock of that pleasure I have never since forgot,
and if my mind serves me to the last, I never shall; for it
was then that I knew I loved reading.

ROSA QUO LOCORUM

Every now and then the Scottish psyche tears itself away, hic-
cuping and reeling from its preoccupation with Burns
Suppers and tries to remember that Scotland produced other
authors worth celebrating. In October 1974, for instance, I
attended a grand Robert Fergusson Supper in the Students
Union of Edinburgh University, to mark the bicentenary of that
great Edinburgh poet's death nearby, in Bedlam.

I am also in the pleasant position of being able to date
exactly the commencement of my special interest in Robert
Louis Stevenson — Thursday, November 18, 1976. I can even
give the hour — sometime between 10.30 am and 11.30 pm.
The place: the ballroom of the Royal Hotel, Bridge of Allan,
near Stirling, in Scotland, at a Literary Evening by the National
Trust for Scotland and the Saltire Society to mark the 126th

anniversary of his birth five days earlier.

A plaque outside claims proudly that Stevenson stayed there in the months of April and May 1867. (It was during 1862 — briefly — as a boy of eleven and he stayed much oftener at the Queen's Hotel!).

The Literary Evening was a *sucess fou*. Our guest speaker was Dr Ian Campbell, of Edinburgh University. I recall at one point reading 'Thrawn Janet' to the assembled throng by candlelight. I waved my script so near to some candles at one dramatic moment that a thoughtful friend slipped out and doused them. Thus was I saved from a fiery climax matching Janet's own.

Afterwards Mrs Ella Maclean, our elderly local historian, informed me that Stevenson had stayed in my house. And she verified this with a statement in 'guid black preent'.

I walked home on air. We had lived in a flat in 'Bellnoir' in Henderson Street for twelve years, but we had never known that! It transpired, however, that Mrs Maclean's source had been wrong. The Stevensons in Bellnoir were his cousins, David and Charles Stevenson while Louis had been with his parents along Henderson Street at Darnley House. I felt I had to check everything else about his many visits to our spa between 1853 and 1875 including the local press lists of visitors, local histories, Mrs Margaret Stevenson's diary, Stevenson's letters, relevant verses and essays.

Eventually I built up a picture of two key figures in his life in Bridge of Allan: Dr Alexander Wilkie Paterson and 'the hunchback druggist of Bridge of Allan' Gilbert Farie.

These proved to be major characters in their own right, involved in an internecine feud which I believe, involved Louis as small boy, youth and young man. There is no space here to spell it all out or try to prove anything. Suffice it to say I think I knew where Stevenson found his inspiration for his Jekyll — and his Hyde!

Stevenson in Bridge of Allan inevitably led to Stevenson in Edinburgh and there, too, I seemed to discover things that no one else had noticed. Stevenson's childhood is of immense importance for an understanding of the adult writer. Not only because of *A Child's Garden of Verses* but because even in his adult works, he continually mined that childhood — its fantasies, its play and play-acting — for material.

As late as the 1890s he tells us, in the essay 'Rosa Quo Locorum' of how and where he fell in love with reading. The scene is unmistakeably Bridge of Allan, though he never says so.

His childhood homes are of equal importance. He wrote practically nothing about the house where he was born, hardly surprising since he left 8 Howard Place aged two. He (and many others) did write a great deal about 17 Heriot Row. Ah, but what of the house in-between, the elusive No 1 Inverleith Terrace which the Stevensons occupied between 1853 and 1857?

I found the biographers, having dismissed that house as demolished, had silently forgotten its existence and things that must have happened to child Lou there had been as silently transferred to Heriot Row.

With the aid of a little simple detective work I discovered that No 1 still stood and was still occupied as No.9 Inverleith Terrace. Moreover (when I called) I found the current occupants had established all this quite independently and had incontrovertible proof for an article which I subsequently had published.

I discovered a good deal about the older RLS too, about the (apparently) idle, ostentatiously Bohemian creature who seemed to spend his non-writing time shocking, or trying to shock, New Town society: Evidence, for instance, of a complex romantic situation involving the student Louis, his handsome, brilliant, ill-fated fellow-student Walter Ferrier, and two Mackenzie sisters, Euphemia and Jane, both of whom make fugitive appearances in the essay 'Old Mortality' and elsewhere. Further gleanings of that particular personal drama, I decided, found its way into *Weir of Hermiston*.

Much of Stevenson's literary work represented Life, particularly his own life, transmuted with Art. It became a fixed habit of mine to trace his sources. Often these were embedded in Edinburgh history. Janet M'Clow (Thrawn Janet) turned out to be the wife of a villainous Edinburgh publican, Kenneth McKenzie, involved in the 'Worcester' affair of 1705 (ie: the murder or hanging of unpopular English sailors consequent on the Darien disaster).

Burchell Fenn, the character who provided secret nocturnal transport for the eponymous hero of *St Ives* owed his odd name to an English soldier (Burchell Venn) involved in the Seige of Leith in 1560.

Lord Glenalmond, the cultured and sympathetic judge in *Weir of Hermiston* turned out to be the first Lord Meadowbank, incidentally the first owner occupier of 17 Heriot Row while Frank Innes, the villain of the same novel, was in fact an Edinburgh gunsmith (Francis Innes) for whom Stevenson's grandfather acted as apprentice in the 1780s.

The description of Essendean, the village from which David Balfour emerged in *Kidnapped,* fits Sorn in Ayrshire, an exact match for the village where Stevenson's other grandfather Dr Lewis Balfour was minister from 1806—23. The Balfours, including Stevenson's mother, liked to go there on visits years later. But Reverend Mr Campbell, the Essendean minister in the novel, was in reality a witness to the purchase by Thomas Stevenson of 17 Heriot Row; a transaction occurring in Campbeltown.

Tombstones or headstones were a great source of character names for the lad who frequently idled in graveyards as a student skipping classes. Adam Weir in *Weir of Hermiston* he plucked off a stone in the Old Calton Cemetery. McKellar (narrator of *The Master of Ballantrae)* came from a minister's tombstone at Kirkmichael encountered while making notes for the novel on his way to Braemar from Moulin in 1881. ('In memory of the late Alexander McKellar, for 17 years Minister in this parish. Died 1866).

Houses Stevenson knew intimately, he used. Glenalmonds' dining room in *Hermiston* was of course the Stevenson's own in Heriot Row. Swanston Cottage featured as itself in *St Ives.* Drumcliffe in Murrayfield where Lou played as a boy, provides a macabre setting for murder in 'The Misadventures of John Nicholson'. Cammo House in Cramond may well be the

House of Shaws in *Kidnapped*.

I mentioned previously the significance of play. Playing at Jacobites and Redcoats by the Allanwater with his cousins, Henrietta and Willie Traquair, may have planted the seeds of *Kidnapped*. Willie possessed a Balmoral bonnet which Lou (the leader) kept pre-empting, we're told. The three were at Bridge of Allan together and probably played on the eyot where the Allan flows into the Forth, on which Alan Breck and David skulk a whole day in view of Stirling Castle.

Glencorse Kirk appears as itself, (transported from the Pentlands to the Lammermuirs) in *Hermiston*. So does its frail old minister Mr Torrance who is buried in the Kirkyard.

But how did all this change my life? Well it certainly became an obsession. That must be obvious. The relations between Stevenson's Art and his Life are complex in the extreme and provide the literary amateur detective with a career for life if he submits to their fascination.

Stevenson's 'borrowings' from history, person, family, national and Edinburgh, of names, houses, places, incidents were sometimes innocuous enough. But there are times when the truth could be a profound embarrassment for he was in the sensitive position of depending a great deal on real life material for his fictions. He wished to weave intimate details of family and personal history into these and in so doing he had to learn to disguise these facts. He became, in consequence, an expert at telling and not telling the truth — simultaneously and inextricably.

Anyone who does not understand this complex aspect of Stevenson does not understand the man. You can never, of course, find the absolute truth about him or his life. He was too skilled a coverer of tracks for that. But you see enough, if you look long enough, to keep travelling on and on, down that teasing devious trail.

And you know what Stevenson wrote about 'travelling hopefully....'

(David Angus died in January 1994 and this essay is published with the consent of Mrs Jean Angus.)

Robert Lawson Watt

BORN: LEITH, 1932. EDUCATION: LEITH, & HERIOT WATT UNIV · B.SC (HONS) · WORKED AS: LAB BOY, SOLDIER, RESEARCH CHEMIST, WORKS MANAGER, COMPANY DIRECTOR · TEACHES CHEMISTRY · WEEKLY COLUMN IN EDINBURGH EVENING NEWS

OTHER WRITINGS INCLUDE EDINBURGH EXPERIENCE, AN EVENING IN SAMOA, SACK 'EM UP MEN IN COLINTON KIRKYARD AND LORD COCKBURN'S BIRTHDAY · HAPPILY MARRIED WITH THREE CHILDREN

RLS and The Leith Man

RLS & THE LEITH MAN
ROBERT LAWSON WATT

We sail in leaky bottoms and on great and perilous waters; and to take a cue from the dolorous old naval ballad, we have heard the mermaids singing, and know that we shall never see dry land any more. Old and young, we are all on our last cruise. If there is a fill of tobacco among the crew, for God's sake pass it round, and let us have a pipe before we go!

VIRGINIBUS PUERISQUE:

CRABBED AGE AND YOUTH

On May 10 1944 I presented myself to the District Commissioner. The place was not some mosquito-dunged corner of the Empire — it was, although I did not know it at the time, a house a few yards from Robert Louis Stevenson's birthplace and the Commissioner was about to test from my Boy Scouts Reader Badge.

Up to that point in my 11 year old life I had not succeeded in anything but RLS was about to change that. I was a black hole when it came to reading. Mr Gloag the Commissioner, looked at my 30 book reading list for a long time. In retrospect it must have appeared precocious, containing titles like 'Soviet Policies for Far Eastern Peoples'. I had instinctively placed a few rafts penned by RLS, *Kidnapped, Treasure Island* enabling Mr Gloag to talk his way across my tome-infested list. Although I did not come from a bookish background, never having discussed a book with anyone until that day, my young instinct told me everybody had read Stevenson. I was awarded my badge and from then the Commissioner nicknamed me 'Reader'.

Shortly after this the film *Dr Jeckyll and Mr Hyde* arrived in Edinburgh. I plunged into the potent portion by paying sixpence and sitting in the warm darkness of the Capital picture house.

Wartime, no ice cream, no popcorn, no sweets, no distractions except the odd air raid, but not that night. First the wee film, next the community singing. With Richard Telford, the famous Edinburgh organist's notes on our ears: 'Run Rabbit Run', the curtains hissed back. Ingrid Bergman laughed at Mr Hyde; he, the fool, bashed her about. The cinema beam cut through the smoke filled air, a lighthouse rose from my loins, a virgin erection, the light from which still pleasures me. RLS's words helped to transmute me from boy to man. Edinburgh is in essence Presbyterian yet it is not obvious to an outsider that its citizens are conceived immaculately. RLS's Mum and Dad did not appreciate his early experiments. My parents, although born 100 years later shared the same light. For us Burns was bonny but never bawdy, we had the translation by numbers from our dictionary for the Burns prize. Not for us discussion of the nuances of 'Coming Through the Rye'. To paraphrase Stevenson's words: Books and films are good enough in their own way but they are a bloodless substitute for life.

Like RLS I left Edinburgh. Like RLS I have certain talents which allowed me to be educated up to a certain level, once this had been achieved, nurture cut off and south I went. I must confess I was not in touch with him over the next 30 years of so. My fault entirely. Elbowing my way up the ladder to increase the crust size for my family and enjoy myself, I kept in touch with books, letters and articles sporadically, while the occasional postcard in the guise of a film or TV documentary kept me aware.

Even the nature of the world had become more Hyde than Jekyll. In 1945 Belsen's barbed wire curtains were pulled aside to reveal horrors beyond Hyde's mind, or on that bright, bright day when the news of the public atomic *flash* declared us victors after five years of blackout and war. It was only when our eyes stopped watering we realised the world would never be the same again for winners or losers. Hyde was out for ever.

More and more Stevenson's insights are leeries on a journey; 'old and young we are all on our last cruise', that erosion from youth to crabbed age. As well as being our last it is also our first and I am not sure the world has crabbed or if it's just my window becoming weather honed.

I returned to Edinburgh but did not renew our acquaintance until a mutual friend brought us together. I was passing our friend's place when I saw her in a bad way, her famed dark brown colour was grey in parts, neighbours had injured her skin with bruised hues, blue nylon ropes a-floating, cola cans with plastic sails a-boating — our beloved friend the Water of Leith was being abused. In a series of serendipitous jumps aimed at river resuscitations, transfusions were administered. First, a photographic exhibition 'From Hills to Sea' starring the Water of Leith produced by John Cruickshank, an Edinburgh photographer. The pictures are superb but something was needed to serpentine the images. Quotations from *A Child's Garden of Verses* provided the weft for the river bed.

The exhibition spawned a number of outcomes and in the last two years regular clean-ups have been organised by the City Council with the result that our friend is looking much more like her old self. As the exhibition was due to close, Mainstream Publishers launched a facsimile edition of *A Child's Garden.* I was approached by Robert Stevenson Club who wanted to use the pictures as a tapestry in Waterstones windows, a publicity slipway for the launch.

I agreed to deliver the images. As I donkeyed the folio around the town on a warm June in 1990, 'The Edinburgh Experience' started to germinate in my head. The idea was simple. I wanted a group of people to meet RLS in a place where he was happy: Vailima. Non-positive thinkers might feel that as he died nearly 100 years ago, it might be difficult to realise my idea. Not a bit of it, you should never believe what you read in the papers. I know that reports of his demise were very much exaggerated.

In a 'somebody up there like me' coincidence, the solution

was at hand; in the hothouses of the Royal Scottish Botanical Gardens, a rainforest had just been built and this provided a youthful Vailima. RLS had to be a bit special, he was not an actor playing a part on a stage, he was RLS hosting a party of visitors from his home town. He had to be Louis for the evening. That fine Stevensonian actor John Shedden was the broonie. Food and wine were authentically researched and prepared, although I must confess that though a young pig was available, the Keeper of Garden felt that digging a pit and lopping bits from the three palm trees for fuel could cause problems with the gardeners. This limited our cooking pot. Music was taped in Samoa and flown across half the world. The guests stepped from a dark winter night into Samoan warmth and were invited by Louis to share a meal with him.

Many of the people present were members of the Stevenson Club so their knowledge of the man would be greater than the average punter. Louis and I agreed that if the evening were to be a success at least five people would have to pass the comment 'He came alive.' Louis did just that, from the first staggery notes of his tin whistle to the conch call of the time-tide ferry, Louis was what he has always been, a superb host. Words, stories, gurgled as fresh as ever. The evening passed the test with pleasure to spare, confirming my experience that as a flying carpet across time, geography and any of man's seven ages, RLS is hard to beat.

After this involvement with RLS, I heard from Elizabeth of the intended celebrations in Samoa in 1994 and I have been asked to help organise a trip to Vailima. You get one chance and that only roulettes every 100 years so I will be there. I intend to sit with the hunter on his hill, pass the time of day with him then catch the wind and go right round the world.

The last words I leave to Louis: 'Make one brave push and see what can be accomplished in a week.'

W Gordon Smith

HAS NEVER LIVED MORE THAN A COUPLE OF MILES FROM STEVENSON'S EDINBURGH HOMES IN OVER 60 YEARS · HAS NO WISH TO LIVE ANYWHERE ELSE · CHAIRMAN OF THE RLS CLUB

PLAYWRIGHT, CRITIC, BROADCASTER · COLUMNIST, SONGSMITH, PHOTOGRAPHER, ARTISTIC DOODLER · TIPPLER AND BELLYGUTSER — MORE OR LESS IN THAT ORDER

By the Light of a Clear Moon

BY THE LIGHT
OF A CLEAR MOON

W GORDON SMITH

*Youth is the time to go flashing from one end of the
world to the other, both in mind and body; to try the
manners of different nations; to hear the chimes at midnight; to see sunrise in town and country; to be
converted at a revival; to circumnavigate the
metaphysics, write halting verses, run a mile to see a
fire...*

CRABBED AGE AND YOUTH

He was such a convivial man. And only a very civilised man
would have had a fatal stroke while making mayonnaise.
Curiously cultivated. Dreamy. He must have seemed 'sensitive' — such a genteel Scottish euphemism — to those who
saw how easily his spirit could be wounded, who heard him
scream against shadows in the night and twiggy fingers
scratching on his windowpane.

Oh aye, a delicate and sensitive boy, all right, yon boy who
wanted more than anything else to be a soldier. Such a contradiction in a man's world. So the boy who became the man
became a paradox. Feet on the ground, head in the clouds.
Physically fragile, tough as old boots. Travels wi' a donkey, did
ye say? Steerage from hither to yon. Riding railroads while
they were still being laid. Knapsacking, footslogging, sailing
before the mast, below the waterline, from woolly west to can-
nibal country.

When I'm eye-boggled tired and invention deserts me, and
the winking insistence of the cursor on my word processor

numbs me to funk, it's then I think of his predicament in a dark room at Hyères. He has damaged his back frolicking like a bairn round a bonfire. His right arm, his writing hand, is strapped to his body to placate a fresh haemorrhage. Drawn blinds reduce the pain of opthalmia. In this inspissated gloom, a board balanced across his knees, he finds the will and purpose, summons creative energy from somewhere, opens the ample cupboard of his mind and like a kind uncle fetches down for us the spiky jingles and divine nonsense of *A Child's Garden of Verses*.

> *Whenever the moon and stars are set*
> * Whenever the wind is high,*
> *All night long in the dark and wet,*
> * A man goes riding by.*
>
> *Late in the night when the fires are out,*
> * Why does he gallop and gallop about?*
> *Whenever the trees are crying aloud,*
> * And ships are tossed at sea,*
>
> *By, on the highway, low and loud,*
> * By at the gallop goes he.*
> *By at the gallop he goes, and then*
> * By he comes back at the gallop again.*

Women love him. They loved him all his life and he loved them back, and for reasons that are daunting and mystical and wonderful, he is still loved, and him a hundred years dead. Handsome, of course, and vulnerable enough to need mothering. Wayward enough to thrill. Fey enough to be fugitive. Worldly wise enough to know how to please a lover. And lavish with honey and blossom and words that tingle the secret places.

> *I will make you brooches and toys for your delight*
> * Of bird song at morning and star-shine at night.*
> *I will make a palace fit for you and me*
> * Of green days in forests and blue days at sea.*

Yet another paradox. The essential woman's man who is out-and-out a man's man. Try getting a bus ticket between him and Charlie Baxter. What a bluidy pair. Archetypally pally. Hands, hearts, drouths — across multitudinous seas incarnadine.

> *A mile an' a bittock, a mile or twa,*
>   *Abune the burn, ayont the law,*
> *Davie an' Donal' and Cherlie an' a',*
>   *An' the mune was shinin' clearly!*

He had an uncanny grip on the core of Scottish character, that kernel of idiosyncracy which betrays national identity beyond peradventure. He laughed and linked arms with it, joined in, roared approval, yet reserved to himself the caveat of a man who looked at wider worlds, understood other cultures, kent other faithers, and learned to adjust perspectives.

Not a professional Scotsman then or now. Any capital he made out of his tribal ancestry had nothing to do with Walter Scott accretions — kilts and chieftains and adjustments of history. Yet few Scottish writers before or since so accurately and economically caught the essence of race in voice or posture. 'Thrawn Janet' gave that old Doric word terrible and eternal definition. There is Old Testament horror too in his tale of two sisters in *Edinburgh: Picturesque Notes* who fell out with such awesome finality that they drew a line through the middle of the floor of the one room they shared and never again spoke a word to each other.

Treasure Island's testament of all-consuming human greed has always smelled and sounded like a Scottish morality, although its participants believed they came from some other part of the planet. And *Jekyll & Hyde* is the ultimate Edinburgh story, the parable of Deacon Brodie — respected burgher by day, cat-burglar by night — who got his comeuppance on his own gallows. The citizen's duplicity personified the city's duality and became a universal metaphor for both. Nothing in our literature matches the horror at the heart of his unfinished masterpiece *Weir of Hermiston*.

I salute him as Tusitala, the teller of tales. Never a day goes by that I do not envy his supple grace as a stylist. From what inspired facility of the mind did he so surely pluck the right words, so elegantly craft the glittering image? I do not envy him his nightmares, his rickety body, his fidgety spirit.

I wish I had known him, caroused with him, laughed, and joined in the choruses until the sun came over the rim of the world

> *Twa o' them walkin' and crackin' their lane,*
> *The mornin' licht cam' grey an' plain,*
> *An' the birds they yammert on stick an' stane.*
> *An' the mune was shinin' clearly.*

STEVENSON'S INFANCY

FROM HIS MOTHER'S DIARY

Born November 13th, 1850: Well and strong to begin with; sat alone and crept at seven months; walked at eleven months; climbed up eighteen steps without help when he was nine months old. When he was twenty months old some one said of him that he understood pictures better than any child of his age he had ever known.

Sept. 1852: Lou begins to be fond of stories, and sometimes asks to be told about the 'big stick' meaning Cain and Abel. That and Daniel among the 'Growlies' are his favourites.

Oct. 23rd, 1852: Lou knows all the story of Eva and Uncle Tom besides a great many out of the Bible, including the Flood and the burning bush. He remembers them wonderfully well.

Jan. 12th, 1853: Lou said; 'What will follow me, Cummy?' alluding to the last verse of the 23rd Psalm.

Feb. 17th 1853: After Lou went out for his walk he expressed great distress because he had not made 'an elegant bow to Mamma.'

April 3rd, 1853: When I was telling Lou about the naughty woman pouring the ointment upon Christ, he said; 'But Mamma, why did God make the woman so naughty?'

April 15th, 1853; Lou is so happy in dear Grandpapa's house at Colinton Manse that he says he will not go home again.

May 20th, 1853, at Bridge of Allan; The servant in our lodgings thinks Lou should be 'put in the papers' as 'something extraordinary.'

July 24th, 1853: Lou's favourite occupation is 'making a church'. He makes a pulpit with a chair and stool, and reads sitting and then stands up and sings by turns.

August 4th, 1853, at St. Andrew's: Lou is delighted with the views of the Bishop's place and the story of 'Candel Beatel' and the bottle dungeon. He gets a bit of paper tied to a string, and standing on a chair shows the way the man shows the dungeon.

Oct. 1st, 1853: Lou's height is 2ft. 11". He is a great chatterer, and speaks very distinctly. He knows a great many stories out of the Bible, and about half the letters of the alphabet, but he is not as fond of hymns as he used to be.

Dec. 3rd 1853: Lou recited the first four lines of 'On Kindness' in great style waving his hand and making a splendid bow at the end. This is Cummy's teaching.

Dec. 8th, 1853: Lou said: 'I don't like that moon, it has got a bit broken off it.'

Jan. 15th, 1854: Lou was told about *Pilgrim's Progress*, much to his delight.

March 26th, 1854: When I read *There is beyond the Sky*, to Lou, he said: 'But why has God got a hell?' I said 'Are we good or bad people?' Lou: I think you and Papa are good.' I said, 'But what kind of hearts have we?' Lou: 'I think you've got a nice one.'

June 26th, 1854. Lou and I were talking about Heaven and golden harps, and he said: 'But I am afraid I couldn't play nicely on mine.'

Dec. 8th, 1854; Lou said 'You can never be good unless you pray.' When asked how he knew, he said with great emphasis: 'Because I have tried it.'

Dec. 11th, 1854: Lou is improving, but requires to be kept very quiet. When forbidden to run about with one of his cousins, he looked thoughtful for a moment, then threw away a toy he had in his hand, and said with great indignation: 'I can't be bothered with such fiddle-dee- dee and nonsense.'

Dec. 18th, 1854. Lou sits for his portrait in chalk to Mr Archer. When Mr Archer asked him what kind of stories he liked best, Lou said: 'I like parables (a pause) and funny stories, too, you know.'

Dec. 25th, 1854: Lou got a sword for his Christmas present. When his father was disparaging it, he said: 'I can tell you, Papa, it's a silver sword and a gold sheath, and the boy's very well off, and quite contented.'

Jan. 1st, 1855: Dear Little Lou very well indeed just now; he neither coughs nor wheezes.

Jan. 9th, 1855: When made to wear his shawl above his sword he was in great distress for fear he would not look like a soldier, and then said: 'Perhaps it will look like a *night march*, Mamma.'

Jan. 16th, 1855; Cummy was climbing the ladder to-day to hang up Dicky, and told Lou to hold it for fear it gave way, and he began to say: 'It's too heavy, it's too heavy,' but he did not let go his hold even when he got his nose bled. Indeed, he clutched at Cummy's gown to keep her from falling.

Jan. 18th, 1855: Lou snibbed himself into the nursery to-day, and we could not get the door opened till Mr Hunter (the wright) came, and took out the panel. Lou was very good as long as any one spoke through the door to him, but cried whenever we tried to get him to open it. When he got out he said he was afraid he would never get out any more, but would 'just be lost.'

Jan. 22nd, 1855: Lou has taken a great fancy to the parable of the vineyard let out to the husbandmen, and can repeat it perfectly from hearing it read.

Feb. 6th 1855: Lou dreamed that 'he heard the noise of pens writing.'

Feb. 7th, 1855: When I asked Lou what story he would like read, he said: 'Oh, you may read the ninth story of John — that's about the man who was born blind, you know.'

Feb. 15th, 1855: Lou is quite mad on the subject of soldiers and war. He prays night and morning for 'our poor soldiers who are fighting at Sebastopol, and may they get the victory.' This is quite of his own accord.

Feb. 23rd, 1855: Lou said: 'Mamma, how can God give us his Holy Spirit, and yet be good Himself?' He also said: 'I am often sorry in the night when I think of all that the Jews did to Jesus.'

May 9th, 1855: Lou was naughty to-day, and after he went to bed he said to Cummy: 'I would like to be good. I think I must say my prayers more *earnestly,* but if I forget it will you do it for me?'

June 16th, 1855: Lou said: 'Am I to get a sweetie every night? I thought I heard a *slight voice* of it.'

Sept. 1st, 1855: Lou's poetry:

> No sun is in the sky
> While night comes on.
> Then stars and moon come out
> And then another day
> The sun comes out again.

Jan. 17th, 1856: Lou's prayer: 'Oh, Lord if it seems good to you, let me have a new brother or sister, if you think proper.'

Feb. 5th, 1856: Dear, wee Lou prayed among other things 'that God would be very near every person that was not very well.'

Feb. 23rd, 1856: When I asked Lou what he had been doing, he said: 'I have been playing all day; at least I have been *making myself cheerful.*'

Feb. 23rd, 1856: Lou said, when walking with his father: 'I'll show you another thing I want to know the meaning of, and that's why they put soda-water bottles on the telegraph.'

Feb. 24th, 1856: I said something to Lou about Christ having died to save him, and he said: 'Did he die to save me?' 'Yes' 'Me?' 'Well, then, doesn't that look very much as if I were saved already?'

April 18th, 1856: Lou can't understand the days getting longer, and says he 'would rather go to bed at the seven o'clock *that used to be.*'

Nov. 23rd, 1856: Lou begins to-day to dictate a history of Moses, to try for a prize which Uncle David is to give for the best.

Nov. 26th, 1856; Lou has inflammation of the cheek; it is terribly swollen, and he suffers so much that he tells me 'perhaps he may never be better.'

Dec. 21st, 1856: Lou finishes his history of Moses, he dictated every word himself on the Sunday evenings.

Dec. 25th, 1856. Lou gets a Bible picture-book as a prize for his Moses, and is greatly charmed. When he got it, he said: 'But I don't deserve it.'

Sept. 30th, 1857: Dear Lou goes to Mr Henderson's school in India St., from ten till twelve o'clock. He says: 'Mr Henderson is the most nicest man that ever was.'

Jan. 10th, 1858: Lou says: 'The churches are much to blame for not sending missionaries to convert the Arabs, Mamma.' Mamma: 'But if people won't go, what can the churches do? Will you go when you're big?' Lou: 'I think you've forgotten one word that was needful.' Mamma: 'What is that?' Lou: 'If I'm spared!'

Jan. 18th, 1858: To-day Lou drew a picture of Sir Henry Havelock praying, which he sent to David Alan before his Papa had seen it. When he heard that I was vexed he drew two others, but neither was so good as the first. The next time I saw him, he said: 'I am blamed for kindness, and get no encouragement for endeavour.'

Feb. 6th, 1858: When I went into the nursery at midnight, Lou was wide awake, and said: 'You see, I have very bad nights. I am always thankful when the morning comes.'

PART II

STUDENT & LOVER
('VELVET COAT')

DAVID DAICHES

BORN: 1912 · EDUCATION: GEORGE WATSON'S, EDINBURGH UNIV & OXFORD · CBE. MA DPHIL (OXON) PHD (CANTAB) FRSL, FRSE · ACADEMIC POSITIONS INCLUDE OXFORD, CHICAGO, CORNELL, CAMBRIDGE, SUSSEX AND EDINBURGH

PUBLICATIONS INCLUDE ROBERT LOUIS STEVENSON; A REVALUATION; ROBERT LOUIS STEVENSON & HIS WORLD; EDINBURGH PICTURESQUE NOTES (ED) · HONORARY DOCTORATES INC THE SORBONNE AND BOLOGNA) · AUTHOR OF OVER 40 BOOKS OF LITERARY CRITICISM, HISTORY, BIOGRAPHY

A LIFETIME WITH STEVENSON

A LIFETIME WITH RLS

DAVID DAICHES

The ancient and famous metropolis of the North sits overlooking a windy estuary from the slope and summit of three hills. No situation could be more commanding for the head city of a kingdom; none better chosen for noble prospects. From her tall precipice and terraced gardens she looks far and wide on the sea and broad champaigns... But Edinburgh pays cruelly for her high seat in one of the vilest climates under heaven. She is liable to be beaten upon by all the winds that blow, to be drenched with rain, to be buried in cold sea fogs out of the east, and powdered with snow as it comes flying southward from the Highland hills. The weather is raw and boisterous in winter, shifty and ungenial in summer, and a downright purgatory in the spring. The delicate die early, and I, as a survivor, among bleak winds and plumping rain, have been sometimes tempted to envy them their fate.

EDINBURGH: PICTURESQUE NOTES

Stevenson more than once professed a sense of identity with the eighteenth-century Scottish poet Robert Fergusson, going so far as to declare 'I believe Fergusson lives in me.' While I can hardly claim that my feeling for Stevenson is quite that of his for Fergusson, I can say that I have long been aware of a similarity in our fortunes and emotions. Both of us combine a

deep love for Edinburgh (where we both grew up) with a long
exile from it and a discovery in exile of the depth of that feeling. Both of us admired and loved our fathers but quarrelled
with them on religious grounds, and both of us went to
America because of a marriage that upset our parents and
returned eventually to Scotland to a warm reconciliation.

When I first read Graham Balfour's 'Life of Stevenson' and
Stevenson's letters, and even more after I had read JC Furnas's
pioneering biography, 'Voyage to Windward', I kept seeing
myself again and again. Not that I claim to have Stevenson's
genius, but his life, his personality, his ambitions, his feelings
and (except in the matter of health) his circumstances seemed
to intertwine with my own. This developed on top of an early
love of his writings. When I was seven my mother gave me for
my birthday a copy of *A Child's Garden of Verses* which I read
avidly again and again,and our teacher in Class D of George
Watson's made us learn 'The Lamplighter' poem by heart. I
too used to see the lamplighter go by with his pole early on
winter evenings, and I knew exactly how the young Stevenson
felt. Edinburgh in the 1920s, when I was a boy, was still
remarkably similar to the Edinburgh of Stevenson's boyhood,
and the middle-class home, the imaginary adventures, the love
of travelling in trains, the sense of the difference between the
seasons with 'Something bright in all', were all familiar to me. And
then I read *Treasure Island* with total absorption and after
that *Kidnapped* in which as a ten or eleven year old I discovered with enormous excitement the importance of a sense of
place, of Scottish topography, of character difference between
Highlander and Lowlander (the reconciliation between David
Balfour and Alan Breck after their quarrel moved me enormously). In my adolescence I read Stevenson's essays and
pretentiously announced to my family that his essays represented Stevenson's greatest achievement.

Then, when I was in the sixth form of George Watson's, our
English teacher the great H J Findlay, introduced us to *Weir of
Hermiston,* reading it aloud to the class during the last two
weeks of the summer term when serious work was over, all
the examination marks were in, and the class could relax. I

was bowled over by it: the difference in character between father and son, the setting alternating between Edinburgh and the grey hills to the south, the interplay of sensitivities and perceptions, the cunningly manipulated shift in the reader's sympathy towards the insensitive and overbearing father, the splendid dialogue between father and son where the father's scornful Scots and the son's apologetic genteel English spell out a whole psychological drama — all this moved me deeply. I was sixteen at the time and by now a committed Stevensonian.

The next phase in my relation to Stevenson took place several years later in America. When I was teaching at the University of Chicago, I was asked by the Head of the English Department if I would like to conduct a graduate seminar on Stevenson. No one at a Scottish university in those days would ever have thought of such an idea, and I marvelled at its boldness. Of course I agreed to do it, and prepared myself by a careful reading, in chronological order, of all of Stevenson's works, including the letters, and at the same time reading all the biographies I could get hold of. The seminar discussed the style and structure of the essays, the movement and pattern of the novels, and traced the psychological conflicts that ran through all of Stevenson's work. It was for me (and I hope for the students) a most rewarding experience.

Word that I was conducting this seminar, and presenting Stevenson as a 'modern' writer, reached the ears of James Laughlin, head of the publishing firm New Directions, and he asked me if I would write a book on Stevenson for his 'Makers of Modern Literature' series. (I had already written a book on Virginia Woolf for the same series). I agreed and the result was 'Robert Louis Stevenson: A Revaluation' first published in 1947.

Reading Stevenson in Chicago evoked in me a great nostalgia, so that I entered into Stevenson's yearning for Scotland when he was in America and later, when he was settled in Vailima, with special intensity. I noted how this was stressed in his last letters to Charles Baxter and other Edinburgh friends, and how the unfinished *Weir of Hermiston* (with its dedicatory nostalgic poem about his native city and its environs) provided him with an 'objective correlative' for his feelings for Scotland. The Americans see an American Stevenson and of course they are quite right to do so since their country played such an important part in his life, both personally and as a published writer. There are memories of Stevenson in California and elsewhere that are real and vivid, as are his own description of his journey *Across the Plains* to find his future wife and his graphic account of his California days. And it was America that gave him his first real fame as an international writer. Yet he was a Scottish writer, and what I have called elsewhere 'the great homecoming of his imagination' in his last months is given memorable expression. I found myself almost overwhelmed by this in reading Stevenson at this time.

Shortly after the publication of my 1947 book on Stevenson I was fortunate enough to meet J C Furnas when he was working on 'Voyage to Windward' and to have many long talks with him. His biography was the first to use the recently released Savile Club letters, and he was able to throw new light on many hitherto misinterpreted details of Stevenson's life. Through Furnas I met the millionaire bibliophile E J Beinecke, whose great collection of Stevenson books and manuscripts were presented to Yale University Library. I had the privilege of opening the Beinecke Stevenson Library at Yale in, I think, 1950 with a lecture on 'Stevenson and the Art of Fiction.'

My connection with Stevenson acquired a new dimension when, after my father's death at the end of the war, my mother bought a flat in Heriot Row (where my brother now lives) a few doors away from No 17, Stevenson's home. On the numerous occasions when I stayed with my mother I could explore that part of the New Town of Edinburgh that Stevenson knew so well, catching those glimpses of the Forth and the shores of Fife as I looked down the streets that ran north from the corners of Heriot Row that were among the vistas celebrated by Stevenson in his *Edinburgh: Picturesque Notes,* a book that still speaks to me most movingly and which I edited a few years ago.

So it all started on my seventh birthday in September 1919

with my mother's gift of *A Child's Garden of Verses* (I still have the volume with her inscription to me). The steady growth of my involvement with Stevenson since then has not stopped with my own generation. My daughter Jenni Calder has inherited my fascination with him which has manifested itself in her biography 'R.L.S. A Life Study' and in her edition of several of the novels. Stevenson has become a sort of family institution for us. For me, my interest in Scottish history and topography, in the literature and culture of Scotland and in the relation between fathers and sons in the nineteenth and early twentieth centuries, come together to keep me permanently involved with this writer, who has the ability to cast a special kind of spell.

Stevenson was no plaster saint or happy invalid or precious stylist, though he was seen as all these things at the beginning of this century. He was a novelist of relationships — between characters and places, between generations and above all between the conflicting impulses in human nature. In his life and work the Calvinist and the Bohemian were constantly confronting each other and the result is a body of writing that illuminates the human condition with power and subtlety.

IAIN FINLAYSON

WRITERS' BURSARY FROM SOUTH EAST ARTS, AUTHOR OF THE SCOTS AND TANGIER HE IS PRESENTLY WORKING ON A BIOGRAPHY OF ROBERT BROWNING

BORN: 1945, AYRSHIRE · EDUCATION: LL.B. EDINBURGH UNIV · BIOGRAPHY THE MOTH AND THE CANDLE, A LIFE OF JAMES BOSWELL WAS FOLLOWED BY WRITERS IN ROMNEY MARSH

Photo by Tessa Codrington

THE WHITE RABBIT IN THE BLACK VELVET COAT

THE WHITE RABBIT IN THE BLACK VELVET COAT

IAIN FINLAYSON

*The love of parents for their children is, of all natural
affections, the most ill-starred.*

*It is not a love for the person, since it begins before the
person has come into the world, and founds on an imaginary character and looks. Thus it is foredoomed to disappointment; and because the parent either looks for
too much, or at least for something inappropriate, at his
offspring's hands, it is too often insufficiently repaid.
The natural bond, besides, is stronger from parent to
child than from child to parent;and it is the side which
confers benefits, not which receives them, that thinks
most of a relation...*

*It is the particular cross of parents that when the child
grows up and becomes himself instead of that pale ideal
they have preconceived, they must accuse their own
harshness or indulgence for this natural result. They
have all been like the duck and hatched swan's eggs, or
the other way about; yet they tell themselves with miserable penitence that the blame lies with them; and had
they sat more closely, the swan would have been a duck,
and home-keeping, in spite of all.*

REFLECTIONS AND REMARKS OF HUMAN
LIFE · LAY MORALS. ETHICAL STUDIES

I feel about Robert Louis Stevenson much as Gelett Burgess
felt about a Purple Cow. He hoped never to see one. Ned
Rorem, the American composer, wrote in 'The Nantucket
Diary' in 1981: 'The three biographies of Cocteau which came

out a dozen years ago depicted three separate people. The best of these biographies — (Francis) Steegmuller's — was nonetheless tainted by the author's having once, briefly, been in Cocteau's presence. His whole notion of Cocteau was colored by the incident. A biographer should either have been a friend of his subject, and then compose a memoir, or never have met his subject at all. (The latter term is easy if you're writing about Magellan or Cleopatra, or Stevenson for that matter).

There is a book of personal reminiscences, titled 'I Can Remember Robert Louis Stevenson', a collection of anecdotes, short memoirs and character sketches compiled and edited in 1925 by Rosaline Masson. Some, who had met the living man, taking their cue from the title of the book, charmingly begin: 'I can remember Robert Louis Stevenson...' and proceed to speak kindly, indulgently and — in some cases — regretfully (that they had not paid more attention) about the subject of their memorial or memoir. It is a book of the greatest biographical interest, since most of the contributors were not literary critics but, rather, solid citizens somewhat bewildered by Stevenson but gamely prepared to admit that a genius had walked among them largely unsuspected — as improbably as an angel in a soft shirt or a minor devil in black velvet.

None of us in this book can claim to have met RLS. We approach his dust much as Shelley, respectfully and reverently, comes across the ruins of Ozymandias. We hunt about, sifting the sand for some chips of stone, some further evidence of his mighty likeness. There is more sand than stone. But whenever we scrape out a recognisable fragment — a petrified knucklebone, perhaps — we are immediately in even deeper trouble. Cyril Connolly remarked that we ourselves know more than dead writers. *They* are what we know. That is to say, they inhabit and inform our cultural history and traditions, they stand ineluctably in our way and there is no getting past them. The more we find out, the more Ozymandias-like they become, the more inscrutable. A pair of massive trunkless legs of stone is imposing and intimidating enough: to look upon Ozymandias plain, as once one could have looked on

Shelley — or Stevenson — plain, would be too transfixing, too glamorizing for us now. Stevenson's contemporaries looked upon the living man in the days before his celebrity and thought no more of the matter than we would do when meeting a friend in the street or the pub and casually passing the time of day before hurrying home for tea.

A meeting, now, for the biographer at least, would be fatal. The biographer is likely to be so glamorized or otherwise inhibited by the sight of the living icon that he would go, inevitably, soft. Detumesce, as it might be. A biography is largely a work of the imagination, often as fictional as a novel. A shilling life, according to Auden, will give you all the facts: more likely, today, a twenty-five quid academic lit-crit biography. The facts are scaffolding — but (to quote 'The Master of Vailima' by Tom Pow) 'there are other kinds of scaffolding, father: lives to make as well as save.' The conscientious academic biographer will 'save' the life, another biographer will be more interested in making a 'life'. The biographer-as-archaeologist will kneel forever in sifting sand: the biographer-as-novelist will turn away and seek his subject in human nature.

I once saw Robert Louis Stevenson on television, as a matter of fact. He looked a lot like Alan Rickman playing the ghost of a cellist who returned to comfort his lover, Juliet Stevenson. The film was 'Truly, Madly, Deeply', by Anthony Minghella, and damn me if Rickman wasn't RLS to the half-life, what Tom Pow describes as 'a rickle of shins, shrouded in white, blackbelted as a buccaneer.' Rickman, as the revenant, couldn't get warm enough. In life, RLS couldn't get warm enough. It hardly bears thinking about that in death he is still shivering. The attentions of posterity are sometimes more chilling than warming. Sometimes we dig up or stumble across the long dead and, to revivify them, wrap them in our sentimentality or romanticism. We bundle them up in their former lives, although the clothes no longer fit or the fashions have changed. Dressed up and weighted with unfamiliar clothes, they appear more accessible, individuals we can comfortably deal with and who — at first glance — may be assumed to conform to our desire to own and possess them.

The ghost, of course, flees its own temple. It scuttles off — as I was going to say, for dear life. But its life is no longer habitable, since it has been occupied by squatters, all vocally maintaining their rights and interests in it.

The shade is on the run. He whips round the corner of Advocate's Close perhaps: a flash of ear and whisker, a dark shadow of black velvet coat-tail is all we catch as we pant in pursuit: RLS as Lewis Carroll's white rabbit, running out of time, ears and whiskers hyper-sensitive to the ticking of the body clock running down, no time to stop, no time to sit and think and be confident that there is time to take it easy in the expectation of the long life that most of us take for granted. Stevenson was forever on the move, sensitive and responsive to the demands of a world that had to be mastered and quickly, quickly. It is at this point a biographer senses and follows a train of thought — perhaps it may be useful, maybe not. But at the corner of Advocate's Close, he sees also the quick whisk of a black velvet jacket.

White rabbit: black mole: 'Little gentleman in velvet.' The free-association technique occasionally produces a novel thought, usually an inversion — the black velvet-coated mole burrows deeply, dutifully underground: working regularly and undistractedly. The underground life of Stevenson, one might say. The unconscious cerebration, thoughts tunnelling through the brain, throwing up little casts and hills until, fatally, the last... a psychoanalyst might have something to say about this subterranean or subcranial image. Is there a hint, here, as to why aficionados of Stevenson are guiltily (because they attempt to repress or suppress) fascinated by the idea of Stevenson cruising Leith Walk in his black velvet jacket?

The burrowing mole is a 'little gentleman' but his underground activities keep the soil aerated and fertile: he does not defile the earth. He is dutiful and yet still a creature of dirt and darkness. Just so was Stevenson — the 'shameless Bohemian haunted by duty.' Stevenson regarded himself as a man held in check only by social forces: unleashed, his terrible potential for destructiveness was unlimited — 'A man who lacks but the opportunity to Ruin Empires,' as he himself commented. Here is

the Caledonian Antizyzygy in its purest form. It is this core in
Stevenson, the arena in which, in life as much as in his literary
work, the conflict between wicked energy and virtuous impo-
tence was played out, that interests me personally. My personal image of Stevenson is of the white rabbit in the black
velvet coat: the restless, running figure of the dutiful, somewhat bureaucratic and constantly busy white rabbit and the
black velvet mole under his feet, equally dutiful and busy but
undermining the ground on which he runs. Stevenson's actual wickedness was mild enough, in all conscience. He turned
his back on the traditions of his forebears to become a writer.
Nevertheless, such a defiance was a radical and defiant rejec-
tion of the commonplace virtues of a family he loved. Such
hubris would, inevitably, have to be paid for. Stevenson
worked to pay the price.

We have the works — the Tusitala Collected Edition fits
neatly and modestly — thirty-odd volumes, none as big as a
modern paperback novel — on the bookshelf. A monument,
in — literally — small book, to a dedicated life: a life dedicated to invincible virtue, to Herculean effort. There are all the
words: the sum of Robert Louis Stevenson, the bedrock on
which the airy edifices of biography rest their fragile foundations. This is as near as we can get to the man — though our
knowledge is supplemented by portraits, photographs, holo-
graph letters and manuscripts, the pious platitudes of his
relicts (Fanny Stevenson, Lloyd Osbourne, Belle Strong), and
some first-hand memoirs. I wouldn't give twopence to *meet*
Stevenson: what I would give a shilling for, however, is a few
moments of his voice in ordinary conversation. Not only
Robert Louis's voice, but the voice, too, of Bob Stevenson —
said by most contemporaries to have been even more fascinating to listen to than his cousin's. The single thing that has
always struck me as most extraordinary is the fact that
Stevenson, in Sydney, used a telephone. He is so much a mid-
to-late 19th century figure, that the thought of a telephone
seems absurdly anachronistic. I wish he'd made a phono-
graph record. Tennyson did, so did Browning, and we're glad
to have that high, tinny sound in the archives. I'd dearly have

loved to hear Stevenson telling a joke or spinning a story.

This has been, perhaps, a self-indulgent essay. What it has been — in actuality, is the public spectacle of a prospective future biographer scrambling to find his feet before attempting to collar his subject and frog-march him down the road that looks most likely to end at some terminus where we can finally take leave of one another with the satisfied feeling that on the journey we have come to a mutually satisfactory knowledge of one another — since biography is also, more or less, concealed autobiography. What this essay has aimed to do is show some evidence that I have at least partly assimilated the words of Marguerite Yourcenar who, defining her own biographical principles, remarked: 'All of us tend to seek out not only the writer, who by definition expresses himself in his books, but also the individual, always necessarily manifold, contradictory, and changeable, hidden in some places and visible in others, and finally — perhaps more than the other two — the *persona,* that reflection or shadow which sometimes the man himself... projects as a defense or out of bravado, but behind which the human being of flesh and blood lived and died in that impenetrable mystery which is part of every life.' She was talking of her own writing about Yukio Mishima, but I take her words as a light to illuminate Robert Louis Stevenson who would, I think, have been proud to have written such a passage himself.

BARBARA BURDICK

BORN: BOSTON, MASS., · BECAME CURATOR OF THE ROBERT LOUIS STEVENSON HOUSE IN MONTEREY IN 1969 & THEN OF LARKIN HOUSE AND LA MIRAGE

ARTICLES & RADIO ON STEVENSON AND ASSISTS VARIOUS ORGANSIATIONS · LIVES IN CARMEL, CALIFORNIA

TO MONTEREY WITH LOVE

TO MONTEREY WITH LOVE
BARBARA BURDICK

Now that you have spelt your
  lesson, lay it down and go and play,
Seeking shells and seaweed on the
  sands of Monterey,
Watching all the mighty whalebones,
  lying buried by the breeze,
Tiny sandy-pipers, and the huge
  Pacific seas.

And remember in your playing, as the
  sea-fog rolls to you,
Long ere you could read it, how I told
  you what to do,
And that while you thought of no one,
  nearly half the world away
Some one thought of Louis on the
  beach at Monterey!
    'TO MY NAME CHILD.'
    A CHILD'S GARDEN OF VERSES

They gathered under the old pear and magnolia trees, resting on weathered wooden benches, some reading, others quietly enjoying the garden, the children running among the roses, waiting to visit the house. It doesn't matter that the author was in the old Pacific capital for only three months, or that he never owned the house they are about to enter because the name of Robert Louis Stevenson has worked its magic and these visitors are about to fall under its spell. It's a wonderful place, this old adobe on Houston Street — the French Hotel, where in two bare chilly rooms the author fought ill health and poverty, recorded his travels and waited to be reunited with his love Fanny Osbourne.

The children came with school groups or often, in the summer and weekends, with their parents. Noisy, sometimes complaining as they waited impatiently at the doorway for the tour to begin, I sensed them settle into the story that began in

Scotland moving westwards to California and eventually ending in Samoa where Stevenson had died in 1894. Often they curiously touched the scratch in the large shining mahogany dining table as I told them how Louis' coffin when lifted from the table at the time of his funeral had left a large L shaped letter on the polished surface. Perhaps it was so, perhaps not, but the attention paid to this fascinating detail helped to direct the small ones' emotion from the sadness of the author's death at forty-four.

Before the children and I adjourned to the upstairs portion of the house I knew their naturally exuberant high spirits might not remain in check for the remainder of the tour so I suggested they sound greetings to Mr Stevenson with their footfalls on the worn old wooden steps 'bang-bang..' by way of a 'hello', then they had to be very quiet when they were upstairs and went by his rooms because he might be sleeping. They never could quite believe he had stayed in such a small room without furniture as it was 100 years ago, with only a writing desk but no fires to warm him in the tiny fireplace.

The children wanted to go in and touch the velvet jacket but the State of California allowed no such liberties. 'He must have been very thin' they usually correctly observed. I often had difficulty moving them along the hall to the other rooms. I watched their faces as I talked and thought Stevenson would have enjoyed seeing these children, and wondered if one day they would in turn tell the story to their own children, about the visit this day to 'his' home in Monterey.

Once a year we had our own special version of the 'unbirthday' party on the 13 November, the day that Stevenson had given away to Annie Ide, because she had, unfortunately, her own on Christmas Day. We had a tea party in the garden and the children listened to the voice of another Scotsman, recorded in faraway Edinburgh, Stevenson's own birthplace, reading the words of 'The Document' correct in Scottish Law that had been given to Annie Ide to mark the occasion.

In 1979, the centenary of Stevenson's arrival in California, the house proudly displayed a huge bouquet of flowers and grasses known to have flourished in California and Scotland

100 years ago. I know because I researched and placed each blossom and stalk in the large brass bowl and stood it on the mahogany table; my own tribute to the pleasure Stevenson had given me over the years and also the joy this special house gives to those who pass through its doors.

My first introduction to Stevenson was in Boston where, at the age of four, my first poem recited from memory (before an audience) was 'My Shadow' complete with rehearsed gestures and a black cotton shadow silhouette at my heels. His words accompanied me through my university literature classes and followed me to Monterey when in 1969 (90 years after his incredible 6,000 mile journey), I was given curatorship of the house that bears his name. In 1937 the house was to be demolished. Mrs C Tobin Clark and Mrs Edith van Antwerp of San Franciso funded a restoration project and four years later donated the house to the state of California as a memorial to RLS, with one of the best collections of Stevensonia in the world.

Here are his baby book with a lock of his hair, the 'leaden soldiers' who marched in the land of counterpane, his velvet jacket and flageolet, first editions of his works, photographs and furnishings from Vailima given to the house by Fanny's family. Visitors from all parts of the earth come to view these treasures remembering their own childhood when 'the world was full of a number of things.'

On May 19 1990, 110 years to the day after Louis and Fanny, I was married in Carmel Valley near the site where Stevenson's life had been spared in the fall of 1879. I chose his words for the ceremony, so appropriate for that special day: 'Love makes people believe in immortality because there seems not to be room enough in life for so great a tenderness.'

I cherish the years I have known this wonderful Teller of Tales, as my personal Stevenson saga continues into a new generation, Granddaughter Sarah likes 'My Shadow' too, but really prefers 'to go up in a swing, up in the air so blue.'

I know that RLS will make her life 'happier for his presence', as he has mine.

LLOYD OSBOURNE

AN INTIMATE PORTRAIT OF RLS

STEVENSON AT TWENTY-SIX

It was at the old inn at Grèz-sur-Loing that I first saw Robert Louis Stevenson. I was eight years old, a tousled-haired, bare-footed child who was known to that company of artists as 'Pettifish.' Though I sat at the long *table d'hôte* I was much too insignificant a person to be noticed by this wonderful new arrival, whose coming had caused such a stir.

But after the meal, when we all trooped down to the riverside to see the *Cigarelle* and *Arethusa* — the two canoes that had just finished the 'Inland Voyage' — the stranger allowed me to sit in his, and even went to the trouble of setting up the little masts and sails for my amusement. I was very flattered to be treated so seriously — RLS always paid children the compliment of being serious, no matter what mocking light might dance in his brilliant brown eyes — and I instantly elected him to a high place in my esteem.

While the others talked I appraised him silently. He was tall and slight, with light-brown hair, a small golden moustache, and a beautiful ruddy complexion; and was so gay and buoyant that he kept every one in fits of laughter. He wore a funny-looking little round cap, such as schoolboys used to have in England; a white flannel shirt, dark trousers and very neat shoes. Stevenson had very shapely feet; they were long and narrow with a high arch and instep, and he was very proud of them. However shabbily he might be dressed, he was always smartly shod. I remember being much impressed by his costume, which was in such contrast to that of his cousin, 'Bob,' who had preceded him to Grèz, and whom I already knew quite well. Bob was attired in a tattered blue jersey such as fishermen wore, trousers that needed no Sherlock Holmes to decide that he was a landscape-painter, and wooden *sabots* of the slightly superior order.

All these lads — for they were scarcely more — were gloriously under the spell of the *Vie de Bohème*; they wanted to be poor, improvident, and reckless; they were eager to assert that they were outcasts and rebels.

It was the custom of them all to rail at the respectable and well-to-do; RLS's favourite expression was a 'common banker,' used as one might refer to a common laborer. 'Why, even a common banker would renig at a thing like that' — 'renig' being another favourite word. I got the impression that people with good clothes, and money in their pockets, belonged to a strange race called Philistines, and were sternly to be kept in their place.

RLS always said he hoped to die in a ditch. He must have

dwelt on it at great length, and with all his matchless humor, for, while I have forgotten the details, the picture of him as a white-haired and expiring wanderer is ineffaceably fixed in my mind. It cost me many a pang that such was to be his end while common bankers jingled by in shining equipages, oblivious and scornful. But the tragedy that hung over Bob was even worse. Bob had divided his modest patrimony into ten equal parts, and after spending one of these every year was to commit suicide at the end. I never saw him lay out a few coppers for tobacco without a quivery feeling that he had shortened his life.

Young as I was I could not help noticing that RLS and my mother were greatly attracted to each other or rather how they would sit and talk interminably on either side of the dining-room stove while everybody else was out and busy. I grew to associate them as always together, and in a queer, childish way I think it made me very happy. I had grown to love Luly Stevenson, as I called him; he used to read the *Pilgrim's Progress* and the *Tales of a Grandfather* to me, and tell me stories 'out of his head'; he gave me a sense of protection and warmth, and though I was far too shy ever to have said it aloud, he seemed so much like *Greatheart* in the book that this was my secret name for him.

When autumn merged into early winter and it was time for us to return to Paris, I was overjoyed when my mother said to me: 'Luly is coming, too.'

STEVENSON AT TWENTY-EIGHT

I was ten when my mother left Paris and came to London, to spend several months before sailing for New York on the way to California. RLS was away somewhere, and it was his cousin 'Bob' who met us at Dover, and took us to our lodgings at 7 Radnor Street, Chelsea.

It was a mean little house in a mean little street, and was as dingy and depressing as cheap London lodgings usually are.

When RLS finally came I was conscious of a subtle change in him; even to childish eyes he was more assured, more mature and responsible. I was quite awed by his beautiful blue suit with its double-breasted coat, and the new stiff felt hat he threw on one side; and there was much in his eager talk about 'going to press,' and 'closing the forms,' and Henley 'wanting a middle' about such and such a subject. He was now connected with a new weekly, called *London,* and evidently found the work very congenial and amusing. He was constantly dashing up in cabs, and dashing away again with the impressive prodigality that apparently journalism required. Indeed, he seemed extraordinarily happy in his new occupation, and was full of zest and high spirits.

I was greatly fascinated by the cane he carried. In appearance it was just an ordinary and rather slender walking-stick, but on lifting it one discovered that it was a steel bludgeon of considerable weight. RLS said it was the finest weapon a man could carry, for it could not go off of itself like a pistol, nor was it so hard to get into action as a sword-cane. He said in a tight place there was nothing to equal it, and somehow the impression was conveyed that journalism often took a man into very dangerous places. When he forgot it, as he often did, I was always worried until he returned.

One evening, with a kind of shyness he never outgrew, he produced a manuscript from his pocket, and read aloud 'Will of the Mill.' Though I understood very little of it, its melodious cadence affected me profoundly, and I remember being so pleased with my mother's enthusiasm. RLS beamed with pleasure; he loved to have his work praised; and he put several questions, as he was always wont to do, for the sheer delight of prolonging such previous moments. Unlike most authors, he read aloud incomparably well, endowing words and phrases with a haunting quality that lingered in one's ears afterward. I have never heard any one to equal him: the glamour he could give, the stir of romance, the indescribable emotion from which one awoke as though from a dream.

At Grèz a young Irish painter had once presented a new arrival to the assembled company after dinner, and in doing so had mockingly labelled the various *habitués.* RLS he had described as 'Louis Stevenson — Scotch literary mediocrity.' The phrase had stung RLS to the quick; it was one of the very few slights he kept alive in his memory. I remember that after he had finished 'Will o' the Mill' and was still in the glow of my mother's praise, he murmured something about its not being so bad for 'Scottish literary mediocrity.'

Later he brought a story about a stranger who had taken a train for some commonplace destination, and who, falling into conversation with his talkative and very queer fellow passengers, suddenly discovered that they were a band of would-be suicides.

From this sprang the 'Suicide Club' series which RLS wrote shortly afterward, and which he read aloud to us in our cheerless sitting-room. Although Stevenson enjoyed them hugely he attached no importance to them; it was enough that they filled a few empty columns of *London,* and brought in a few pounds. They attracted no notice whatever, and in the bottom of his heart I believe RLS was just a little ashamed of them. I know at least that when it was suggested a few years later to publish them in book form he emphatically demurred on the ground that it might hurt his reputation.

Meanwhile the hour of parting was drawing near. I had not the slightest perception of the quandary my mother and RLS were in, nor what agonies of mind their approaching separation was bringing; when the time came I had my own tragedy of parting, and the picture lives with me as clearly as though it were yesterday. We were standing in front of our compartment, and the moment to say goodbye had come. It was terribly short and sudden and final, and before I could realize it RLS was walking away down the long length of the platform, a diminishing figure in a brown ulster. My eyes followed him, hoping that he would look back. But he never turned, and finally disappeared in the crowd. Words cannot express the sense of bereavement, of desolation that suddenly struck at my heart. I knew I would never see him again.

STEVENSON AT TWENTY-NINE

Monterey in 1879 was a sleepy old Mexican town, with most of its buildings of sun-dried bricks called *adobe.*

Our home was a small, two-storied, rose-embowered cottage fronting on Alvarado Street; my mother rented it from two old Spanish ladies named Bonifacio*, who lived in an upper part of it in a seclusion comparable to that of the Man with the Iron Mask.

It was here one morning in our sitting-room that my mother looked down at me rather oddly, and with a curious brightness in her eyes, said: 'I have news for you. Luly's coming.'

I think RLS must have arrived the next day. I remember his walking into the room, and the outcry of delight that greeted him; the incoherence, the laughter, the tears; the heart-welling joy of reunion. Until that moment I had never thought of him as being in ill-health. On the contrary, in vigor and vitality he had always seemed among the foremost of those young men at Grèz; and though he did not excel in any of the sports he had shared in them exuberantly. Now he looked ill, even to my childish gaze; the brilliancy of his eyes emphasized the thinness and pallor of his face. His clothes, no longer picturesque but merely shabby, hung loosely on his shrunken body; and there was about him an indescribable lessening of his alertness and self-confidence.

This fleeting impression passed away as I grew more familiar with him in our new surroundings. Certainly he had never seemed gayer nor more light-hearted, and he radiated laughter and good spirits. His talk was all about the people he was meeting, and he gave me my first understanding of the interest to be derived from human nature. That he should visit one of the despised Genoese in hospital, and read aloud to him a newspaper in his own gibberish, at first horrified me; and that he should be seen walking confidentially along the street with the town drunkard and when one night, in all stealth and secrecy, he helped to print and paste up everywhere a small broadside denouncing the Spanish priest, 'Father Two-Bits,' for his heartlessness and rapacity, I was a good deal more overcome I imagine, than the scoundrelly old victim himself. Young as I was I knew how men could be waylaid and stabbed in those unlit streets at night, and I trembled for Luly, and wished he had more sense.

His concluding enormity was to set the woods on fire, and though he was very conscience-stricken about it he had no real-

(*Bonifacio Adobe relocated still exits in Monterey — Ed.)

ization of the summary punishment that might be meted out to him. There was a tradition in Monterey of a man having been lynched for this offence, and my hair nearly stood on end. I shall never forget my relief when he promised my mother, with appropriate solemnity, though with a twinkle in his eyes, that never, never, never so-help-him-God, would he ever let as much as a whisper of this crime pass his lips.

I was old enough to appreciate how poor he was, and it tore at my boyish heart that he should take his meals at a grubby little restaurant with men in their shirt-sleeves, and have so bare and miserable a room in the old *adobe* house on the hill. Conceive my joy, therefore, when one day he burst in with the news of a splendid job, and prolonged the suspense by making us all try to guess what it was; and my crushing disappointment when it turned out to be as a special reporter on the local paper at two dollars a week.

It was supposed to be a joke, and I laughed with the rest; but on my part it was a sad and wondering pretence. Two dollars meant eight meals at the fishermen's restaurant. What was to become of poor Luly, who daily looked thinner and shabbier? But afterward my mother reassured me, and I was thrilled to hear of what 'experience' meant to a writer, and how in reality Monterey was a kind of gold mine in which Luly was prospering extraordinarily, little though he looked it. Then my father came down for a short stay, his handsome, smiling face just a little clouded, and with a curious new intonation in his voice during his long closeted talks with my mother. He was a tall, very fine-looking man, with a pointed golden beard, and a most winning and lovable nature; I loved him dearly, and was proud of his universal popularity.

I had looked forward eagerly to his visit, and it was disconcerting to find him so pre-occupied and with so little time to devote to me. He seemed forever to be talking with my mother in a seclusion I was not allowed to disturb. Once as I was studying my lessons in an adjoining room and felt that strangely disturbing quality in their subdued voices — reproaches on her side and a most affecting explanation on his of his financial straits at the time of my little brother's death — I suddenly overheard my mother say, with an intensity that went through me like a knife: 'Oh, Sam, forgive me!'

I knew nothing of what all this meant until shortly afterward as I was taking a walk with Stevenson. He was silent and absorbed; I might not have been there at all for any attention he paid me. Ordinarily a walk with him was a great treat and a richly imaginative affair, for at a moment's notice I might find myself a pirate, or a redskin, or a young naval officer with secret despatches for a famous spy, or some other similar and tingling masquerade. But this walk had been thoroughly dull; we had remained ourselves, and not a breath of romance had touched us; and Luly's pace had been so fast, besides, that my little legs were tired.

All at once he spoke, and here again was this strange, new intonation, so colorless and yet so troubling, that had recently affected the speech of my elders. 'I want to tell you something.' he said. 'You may not like it, but I hope you will. I am going to marry your mother.'

I could not have uttered a word to save my life. I was stricken dumb. The question of whether I were pleased or not did not enter my mind at all. I walked on in a kind of stupefaction, with an uncontrollable impulse to cry — yet I did not cry — and was possessed of an agonizing feeling that I ought to speak, but I did not know how, nor what.

But all I know is that at last my hand crept into Luly's, and in that mutual pressure a rapturous sense of tenderness and contentment came flooding over me. It was thus we returned, still silent, still hand in hand, still giving each other little squeezes, and passed under the roses into the house.

PART III

THE WRITER
"R.L.S"

JOHN CAIRNEY

MANY STAGE APPEARANCES INCLUDING HAMLET AND MACBETH · WRITER OF FOUR BOOKS & COUNTLESS SCRIPTS · NOW LIVES IN AUCKLAND, NEW ZEALAND WITH ACTRESS WIFE ALANNAH O'SULLIVAN.

BEGAN AT GLASGOW CITIZENS' THEATRE & BRISTOL OLD VIC · TV WORK INCLUDES THIS MAN CRAIG AND BURNS · FILM WORK: RANK, ABPC, HAMMER & COLUMBIA PICTURES

'ALL THE WORLD'S A STAGE...'

72

ALL THE WORLD'S A STAGE
JOHN CAIRNEY

No art can 'compete with life' whose sun we cannot look upon, whose passions and diseases waste and slay us — to compete with the flavour of wine, the beauty of the dawn, the scorching of fire, the bitterness of death and separation — here are, indeed, labours for Hercules in a dress coat, armed with a pen and a dictionary to depict the passions, armed with a tube of superior flake-white to paint the portrait of the insufferable sun.

A HUMBLE REMONSTRANCE

I first met Robert Louis Stevenson, so to speak, in the person of an Aberdeen housewife and mother of two who suggested that I play him as a theatrical one-man show. This was in 1972 and Alanna Knight had yet to achieve her present deserved status as much-published novelist and writer on Stevenson. I was then at the height of my theatrical solo career as Robert Burns, Scotland's National Bard, and was being bombarded from all sides by friends and colleagues with ideas and names for other one-man shows to follow. Subjects suggested included other such different Scots as David Livingstone, Lord Byron, Thomas Lipton and even William McGonagall. Alanna herself at one stage proffered Robert Cunninghame-Graham (entitled 'Don Roberto' in her radio play) as a possible subject. However, it was when 'The Robert Burns Story' was presented at Aberdeen's Her Majesty's Theatre as part of Aberdeen Festival in June 1972 that I was formally introduced by Alanna to the idea of Robert Louis Stevenson as a possible subject for dramatic portrayal.

Like every other Scottish schoolboy I knew the Stevenson of *A Child's Garden of Verses*, (from the BBC Children's Hour), the great adventure stories like *Treasure Island* (from the local library) and *Dr Jekyll & Mr Hyde* (mainly from its film adaptions) but very little else. In 1962 I had played *The Master of Ballantrae* in a BBC Television six-week serial adapted by Pharic McLaren. In 1971, Bill Bryden asked me to play Alan Breck in a stage production of *Kidnapped* at the Edinburgh Royal Lyceum but I was touring with my solo McGonagall at the time. Ironically, around the same time, I tested at Pinewood Studios for the part of Alan Breck in a film being made of *Kidnapped* but lost out to a Cockney — Michael Caine. 'Et moi qui suis originaire de Glasgow'.

It can be seen then that I was hardly a Stevenson authority prior to my fateful meeting with Mrs Knight. I knew little indeed of Stevenson the man, the wordsmith and essayist, and was quite ignorant of his quirky, courageous personality. I knew only that he came from Edinburgh sometime in the nineteenth century and had died in Samoa. The former fact did not entirely endear him to a Glaswegian and the latter semed of little relevance. The Stevenson irony is that I am now as much of a willing expatriate in the South Pacific as he ever was, having been a citizen of New Zealand since 1980. However, ten years before, what added to my doubts about playing him was that Stevenson represented an East of Scotland Presbyterian Protestantism which was at distinct odds with my West of Scotland Irish Catholicity and even more importantly, my well-fed physique was hardly appropriate to the etiolated outline of the legendary R.L.S. In short, I could not have been more wrong in terms of straightforward casting. I was quite prepared to forget the whole thing, but I reckoned without Alanna Knight — and of course Robert Louis Stevenson.

Such are the ways of theatre (and life) that a Stevenson dramatisation did in fact come to pass but not before Alanna and I were made aware of an extraordinary co-incidence. During 1972-3 as we were preparing the script of what came to be known as 'The Private Life and Public Works of Robert Louis Stevenson', Alanna received some household effects from her mother's home in Newcastle. At the very bottom of a

Victorian blanket-box was a black velvet jacket with braid-lined pockets, which was carefully wrapped in yellowing end-of-the-century newspapers. She thought it might be just right for me to wear as the younger RLS and when I gingerly tried it on I found that it fitted like a glove. When we came to check it later against photographs of Stevenson in Edinburgh we found to our astonishment that he was wearing exactly the same black, velvet jacket with black braid-lined pockets. It seems that Alanna's mother had brought the box from Scotland on her marriage. It had been in the family since then but no-one had ever looked at the bottom of the trunk — that is, until I needed a costume. So much for my miscasting. It is on chance events like this that my life decisions are made and I felt in no doubt now that I would not only play Stevenson on stage, but more importantly, I resolved to become involved with him more and more from that time on.

Was it possible — could this ancient, velvet jacket have been Stevenson's? It was not impossible. He was known for his pre-deliction for black velvet and was inded called 'velvet coat' by street urchins during his youth. It was known too that he generally ordered several at a time and this one in question still had the remnants of the original canvas and linen lining. I remember it looked like the material one used to see covering old-fashioned matresses. The garment could feasibly have been left behind at 17 Heriot Row when the house was vacated in the middle Nineties. It was known that the house stood derelict for a period around 1910. Or was it genuinely left behind when Stevenson waved farewell to Auld Reekie after his father's funeral in 1887?

Whatever the provenance of this particular jacket, it was an eerie feeling wearing it. At any rate, I did so proudly at the first performance of Alanna's play at the Arts Theatre in Aberdeen when John Shedden and I played the twin eponymous roles and again when the play was presented during the 1974 Edinburgh Festival at the Lyceum Studio Theatre with my old friend Leonard MacGuire upstaging me superbly as the other Stevenson. The jacket did not help. Nevertheless, I continued to wear it for every performance I ever gave of RLS until the final one at the Edinburgh Book Fair in 1985. However, if clothes maketh not the man, neither does the costume the actor. Incidentally, in 1974, I was exactly the same age Stevenson was when he died — forty-four. At least my timing in that respect was right, although I had certain misgivings about taking over where he left off. I may have been wearing his actual jacket or I may not, but it helped me little in arriving at an acceptable portrayal, although I did do an hour solo as 'Mr RLS' for Calgary Television in 1976. It was not until I toured in my own solo version of the Stevenson story under that title 'Mr RLS' and in the subsquent duo version 'Mr & Mrs RLS' with my actress-wife Alannah O'Sullivan in 1979, that I came anywhere near an acceptable stage performance of this unique and complex man. But I was learning all the time. To add to my own store of Stevensonia, in the April of that year, Mr Arthur Scholy sent me his one-man play based on *Dr Jekyll and Mr Hyde*. Alanna Knight's idea in her original adaption had been to show the two Stevensons' that were in the man himself — the stern, Covenanting Scot rooted in the Bible and the artist man of the world, embedded in flesh. This not only reflectd the famous Jekyll and Hyde dichotomy, but echoed the very Scottish concern with the ongoing war between a man's public front and his private nature. James Hogg had pioneered the same ground with the 'Confessions of a Justified Sinne'r, but Stevenson had been the first to put into into print the full horror of Edinburgh respectability and its demands on the individual personality and character.

The concept also lent itself aptly for discussion of the twin aspects of the theatrical act itself — one man pretending to be another. The symbolism evident in the two masks of theatre. The ultimate question was which was the lie — the mask or the man? This is the paradox that has intrigued critics since Plato (who did not approve of actors and questioned the whole morality of professional pretence) as it also concerned Denis Diderot (1713-84), who admired actors and attempted to evaluate their contributions to the art of the drama, and especially towards a greater unity betwen actor and dramatist.

In my own way I was working towards this ideal in the

solos. By use of this convention I hoped for a greater ease in audience contact in the words used to communicate with them and to allow them to receive the play's ideas, which had been written specifically for me — for my own voice as it were. I had done so with the Burns solo and now with the Stevenson I had to re-adapt the material for this kind of direct frontal performance. At least, I still had the jacket.

The script performed in the American tours and in Hawaii and Sydney is now in the Library and Museum of the Performing Arts in Lincoln Center, New York, as part of the Billy Rose Theatre Collection. The American interest in Stevenson and Theatre is not surprising. Due to his longish stays in Saranac Lake, New Jersey and Silverado in the Napa Valley in California and variously in New York City and San Francisco followed by his later sojourn in Hawaii, many Americans lay a part-claim to Stevenson as an adopted American.

But not even the Americans can deny his essential Scottishness. He never tried to hide this and latterly, as Tusitala on his South Seas island, he may even have enjoyed playing a Polynesian version of the clan chief. Stevenson played many parts in his short life — student rebel, studied bohemian, clubable man, man of letters, inveterate traveller, compulsive sea-farer, professional invalid and amateur musician. Role-playing was an essential part of his complicated make-up and he played the part very well. He enjoyed acting everywhere except upon a stage. If he was a poor performer on the boards he was a natural actor in the drama he played out in life. His theatricality was as valid to his personality as his actuality.

Alanna Knight and I had imagined in 1972-74 that we were the first to research and compile a theatre-piece about Stevenson's life and work using, as far as possible, his own words as text. This was dramatic biography along the same lines I had used as Robert Burns in 1969 but in fact, Mrs Knight and I found that we were part of an on-going Stevenson theatrical industry which had been going on for years and which had no less than Stevenson's own authority for doing so. He recognised before anyone what an important literary, as well as theatrical source lay in the facts of life — anyone's life — and anyway, as he indicates, it makes things easier for the writer:

> I like biography far better than fiction myself. You have your little handful of facts, little bits of a puzzle, and you sit and think, and fit 'em together this way and that, and get up and throw them down and say 'damn' and go for a walk, and it's real soothing; and when it's done it gives an idea of finish to the writer that is very peaceful. Of course, it's not really so finished as quite a rotten novel; it always has, and must have, the incurable illogicalities of life about it... still that's where the fun comes in.

Read any page of the best Stevenson and you are reading compelling theatre. He writes as actors act — aware of the primary and secondary rhythms, on the look-out for words to point or stress or surprise, phrases to relish and others apparently to throw away. Like actor's lines in a good performance, his words skim on the page, darting and winging with absolute certainty into the minds and imaginations of the reader whose only duty is to turn the page for the same reason as the audience's is to sit and listen — for both to believe. Both actor and author are artists at the service of their respective audiences.

Robert Louis Stevenson and I had more than a velvet jacket in common.

ALANNA KNIGHT

BOOKS INCLUDE ROBERT LOUIS STEVENSON TREASURY · RLS IN THE SOUTH SEAS · THE PRIVATE LIFE OF RLS & THE PASSIONATE KINDNESS · LIVES IN EDINBURGH

AUTHOR OF SCOTTISH HISTORICAL NOVELS AND THE INSPECTOR FARO CRIME SERIES · PLAYS/ DOCUMENTARIES INCLUDE RLS'S ACROSS THE PLAINS FOR RADIO

HAPPIER FOR HIS PRESENCE (1)

HAPPIER
FOR HIS PRESENCE (1)
ALANNA KNIGHT

*The task before us, which is to co-endure with our exis-
tence, is rather one of microscopic fineness, and the
heroism required is that of patience. There is no cutting
of the Gordian knots of life; each must be smilingly
unravelled.*

*To be honest, to be kind — to earn a little and to spend
a little less, to make, upon the whole, a family happier
for his presence, to renounce when that shall be necessary and not be embittered, to keep a few friends, but
these without capitulation — above all, on the same
grim condition, to keep friends with himself — here is a
task for all that a man has of fortitude and delicacy.*

A CHRISTMAS SERMON

'There by the cheek of a brisk fire on a cool September afternoon, in the
house lugubriously known as "the late Miss McGregor's cottage," I began the
tale...'

So began my own introduction to Robert Louis Stevenson
who had written those words in Braemar, only 40 miles from
our home in Aberdeen. The book was *Treasure Island* which
I had read in a children's edition to Chris and his younger
brother Kevin as we sailed to Beirut where my husband
Alistair had a fellowship at the American University. Our homecoming a year later was marked and marred for me by the
onset of polyneuritis, a disease of the auto-immune system.
Virtually paralysed for the next six years, with the aid of an
electric typewriter and the support of a devoted family who
refused to let me be hospitalised, I had been learning to be a
writer.

Never was there such a feeling of serendipity, of hope and

faith, as when Stevenson re-entered my life by way of Chris's English project. I had to know more about him. Alistair asked if the University Library had a biography and staggered in behind a yard of books: 'And when you've finished, there are twice as many waiting on the shelves.'

From that day onward I read everything I could lay hands on by or about Stevenson. And as I read, enthralled, I discovered an immediate and strange affinity with this man who had been a frail only child, a chronic invalid and who could put into such perfect words all the feelings I was struggling to express.

I didn't know it then but there were still two trying years of incapacity ahead of me before I was to meet John Cairney. Would I write a play about Stevenson for him? I had never written a play I protested. I wouldn't know where to begin. 'Nothing to it,' he said encouragingly, 'It's easy. You write novels, don't you?'

I did and my first two had been published, but a play was a different matter. In due course 'The Private Life and Public Works of R L S' was written with John staring over my shoulder and using his tremendous knowledge of stage craft to bring it to life.

The premiere was in Aberdeen Arts Centre: John Cairney, John Shedden and Rose McBain in the principal roles. I was duly appointed stage manager and wardrobe mistress. At teatime John phoned from the theatre. Panic. He needed a black cravat as Stevenson's father. We didn't have one. 'But you can make one easily,' John insisted, 'any old scrap of black material will do.'

Upstairs was a seaman's trunk once the proud possession of my captain great-grandfather which had descended via Gran to Mother who had settled it with me. I remembered that, as well as blankets, old curtains and a prevailing smell of mothballs, there were scraps of blackout material from war days. There was also Gran's old chenille tablecloth, perfect to give an authentic touch to the 'Heriot Row' scene. As I dived below lace tablecloths, bolster cases, all carefully wrapped in brown paper, I unearthed what looked at first glance like a chunk of very creased black velvet. I gave it a shake, and it emerged as a once-elegant gent's jacket, its silk lining, worn and torn, the silk braid that edged sleeves, collar and pocket also much the worse for wear, or lack of it, for obviously the jacket had languished in the trunk undisturbed for many years.

After working miracles, from the distance anyway, with a steam iron, the jacket would surely fit a very slender man of medium height. Triumphantly carrying my trophies to the theatre I watched John examining his reflection in the mirror, the perfection of sleeve length and shoulders. Suddenly he shivered. 'Looks as if it had been made specially for me, doesn't it?'

The play applauded, a modest success, when I got home, the phone was ringing. Mother wanted to know, had all gone well? Yes indeed. And that black velvet jacket in Gran's trunk was perfect for John, fitted him like a glove.

There was a pause. 'What jacket?'

I explained again, the bottom of the trunk, the newspaper.

'Well, it certainly didn't come from this house. I know everything that's in Gran's trunk — there's this — and that ' she went into a complete description of every item. 'But there never was a velvet jacket, man's or woman's. That I do know.'

I tried again. Narrow shoulders, braided bits.

Mother sniffed scornfully. 'Narrow shoulders. Then it would never have fitted any of our men, all built like barn doors, over six feet tall, had to have everything made. Besides I've met John Cairney,' she added. But I fancied it was the description of the jacket's scruffy condition and ragged lining that offended her most. 'We've never had anything like that in our house.'

I put down the phone and remembering the lines in the play where Stevenson is called 'Velvet Coat' I took down one of the biographies. And there in the Bournemouth portrait taken in 1887 was the jacket I held, identical to the last detail of collar shape and braided pocket.

John has already described his close encounters with the

'Stevenson jacket', a surprised Glasgow tailor dated it as about a hundred years old. The mystery remains and   we're no nearer knowing where it came from and how it came be waiting for discovery, hours before the play was to open.

The other Stevenson puzzle is even harder to explain. I've talked to biographers and historical novelists who have also had the feeling that their subject was 'looking over their shoulder' as they wrote. And many far from psychic confess to being uncomfortably aware of that 'other presence'. The logical explanation is that when a book is going extremely well, writers often become aware of words pouring out of them and on to the paper, as if in fact something outside themselves is momentarily at the controls of the creative process. Stevenson once said: *the intolerable clatter of a typewriter removes from me all that makes it valuable to a man.* How he would have viewed the word processor!

'The Passionate Kindness' (the book of the play) was followed by a radio adaptation of 'Across the Plains' and I fondly imagined that that was the end of my Stevenson association. Until one day John Cairney on a visit brought his new one-man 'Mr RLS'. As I read I said: 'John, this quotation is *not* Stevenson.' 'Isn't it?' he replied, 'then you had better write me a Concordance— like the one I have for Robert Burns. Then I won't make any more mistakes.'

A four-year labour of love and 'The Robert Louis Stevenson Treasury' published, I wistfully contemplated a return to historical novels, but Louis wasn't finished with me. Having proved myself such a willing and obliging apprentice, he had another task in store. While researching the 'Treasury' I had practically lived in Edinburgh Central Library, (no praise is too great for the patient staff) and one day, a librarian about to retire, presented me with a box of glass slides. Under a century of dust were photographs taken by the Stevenson family during their travels in the South Seas. The writing on them was almost illegible, spidery and brown with age but as I held them I knew I had gold in my hands. Most had never seen the light of day and I was faced with the solving of my first Edinburgh mystery: identifying the photographs and finding the appropriate quotation from Stevenson to accompany them.

'RLS in the South Seas' was published in 1986. And so back to Aberdeen and more novels. But fate had one more card to play. A family holiday in a friend's Edinburgh home and we succumbed to the temptation of a rented flat. A year later we too had fallen in love with Stevenson's 'precipitous city'. As Alistair was about to retire, we exchanged our modern five bedroomed Aberdeen house for a century old Victorian flat.

I had never lived in anything older than 1933 and even stranger was the discovery that there was someone already there, waiting for me to give him life. In no time at all, I had also switched careers and embarked upon a life of literary crime with Detective Inspector Jeremy Faro in the Edinburgh of 1870s. An Edinburgh I was completely at home with, for hadn't I been walking its paths and touching its stones hand in hand with Robert Louis Stevenson for nearly fifteen years?

Six Faro books later and Stevenson had retreated like the once beloved friends of one's youth who depart for distant climes and whose voices are heard no more. Apart from the occasional query from a Stevenson buff or a request for a talk to some learned society, I had said: 'Thank you, dear Louis. I've enjoyed knowing you.'

Then last autumn Elizabeth Stuart Warfel arrived from California on her twice yearly pilgrimage to Edinburgh and this book was conceived.

'And now' as Stevenson said in his preface to *Treasure Island*, 'admire the finger of predestination ...'

TREVOR ROYLE

BORN: MYSORE, INDIA · EARLY CHILDHOOD: MALAYSIA · EDUCATED IN SCOTLAND · MA (ABERDEEN) · ASSOCIATE EDITOR OF SCOTLAND ON SUNDAY NEWSPAPER · BBC RADIO BROADCASTER

AMONG HIS STEVENSON DRAMATISATIONS: THE PAVILION ON THE LINKS AND THE SUICIDE CLUB · BOOKS INCLUDE THE BEST YEARS OF THEIR LIVES, THE LAST DAYS OF THE RAJ & BIOGRAPHIES OF KITCHENER OF KHARTOUM AND GLUBB PASHA OF THE ARAB LEGION

STEVENSON
AND THE RADIO

STEVENSON AND THE RADIO

TREVOR ROYLE

You may remember how Burns, numbering past plea-
sures, dwells upon the hours when he had been 'happy
thinking'. It is a phrase that may well perplex a poor
modern, girt about on every side by clocks and chimes,
and haunted, even at night, by flaming dial-plates. For
we are all so busy, and have so many far-off projects to
realize, and castles in the fire to turn into solid habit-
able mansions on a gravel soil, that we can find no time
for pleasure trips into the Land of Thought and among
the Hills of Vanity... We are in such haste to be doing, to
be writing, to be gathering gear, to make our voice audi-
ble a moment in the derisive silence of eternity that we
forget that one thing, of which these are but the parts —
namely, to live.

> *VIRGINIBUS PUERISQUE.*
> *'WALKING TOURS'*

Had Robert Louis Stevenson been living in the great days of
steam radio he would have been in constant demand as a
scriptwriter. It is tempting far too much, perhaps, to claim
that he would have made his mark either as a presenter or as
that ugly modern manifestation, a 'media personality', but
there is little doubt that producers would have been queuing
up everywhere to commission his services for the written
word.

I can make that claim because it has been my good fortune to have adapted some of his best work for radio, either as dramatisations or as abridgements and on each occasion I have been uncomfortably aware that my hand has been guided by the narrative strengths and rich use of language which inform just about all his work.

Consider the facts. There have been several remarkable adaptations of *Kidnapped* for radio, and why not? It is a splendid yarn which rattles along at a fair old pace; there is adventure aplenty and the novel introduces two of Stevenson's most enduring characters, the solid Lowlander David Balfour and the adventurous Highlander Alan Breck Stewart. Because so many contradictions bind these two men together it would be a dull mind which did not rise to the dramatic tension they create in the midst of so much adventurous action.

When I abridged and adapted the novel for Schools Radio in the early 1980s these conflicting loyalties seemed to take on a greater urgency because only a year or two had gone by since Scotland had been involved in the great devolution debate. At that time self-government, or at least a smidgen of independence, had been within grasp — only to be snatched away by an outrageous display of gerrymandering in Westminster, and the conflict between Balfour's practical Hanoverianism and Alan Breck's romantic Jacobitism was entirely apposite in a radio piece for lively Scottish teenagers. Not for the first time Stevenson's ideas were striking exactly the right kind of note for a later day and age.

I'm not claiming that Stevenson was a crypto-nationalist or that *Kidnapped* contains lessons which can guide us through today's political minefields, but at that moment it seemed no bad idea for the production to point up some of the conflicting interests and loyalties which stalk through Scotland's history.

There are other details which make *Kidnapped* such an extraordinary piece of writing for radio — the lost inheritance, the flight in the heather, the rich tapestry of historical detail — but the characters provide the real bench-mark. Because both are essentially heroic personalities they have attributes which strike a chord in even the most casual listener. (Alan Breck's boastings were a distinct bonus in this respect!) In other words — and this is vital in radio drama — they command an audience's interest. We want to know what will happen to them by the time that the programme comes to an end.

Of course, this is where radio comes into its own because there are no visual images to delight or distract the mind. These have to be created by the power or passion of the words and by the ability of the actors and the producer to breath life into them. In a drama studio the actors have few distractions other than the mute microphone and the small but critical audience of production staff in the adjoining cubicle with its array of recording machines and high-tech gadgetry. Here it's comparatively simple to recreate the wind on the moor and the cry of distant soldiers, or the slow creak of a ship at sea in a soft swell. For the listener, unaware of the electronic wizardry, temporal and spatial boundaries are dissolved and aural suggestion reigns supreme.

For the writer these are indeed miracles. *Treasure Island* can be reached without a lengthy and expensive journey, California and the Silverado Squatters require but a lonesome train whistle to place them, the South Seas come alive in a blaze of effects from the BBC's marvellous sound library. There is no need to limit locations for budgetary considerations and few temptations to confine the size of the cast (within reason) for it is perfectly feasible for actors, hidden from the inquisitive stare of their audience, to double up the speaking parts.

Without making too many grandiose claims for the primacy of radio drama it is fair to say that it is the one area of the media where anything is possible and where true imagination is allowed to run free. In that respect radio production offers a reflection of the creative process itself, rather like 'the pleasant land of counterpane' where 'the world is so full of a number of things.'

Not without reason, given their accessibility and popularity, Stevenson's novels of adventure — *Kidnapped, Catriona, Treasure Island, Master of Ballantrae* — have been a happy hunting ground for the producer anxious to find subject matter for a single radio drama or for the more ambitious BBC

Classic Serial. (Indeed, the process of adapting great literary works has grown to such an extent that radio is one of the principal means by which most people gain access to the literature of the past.) After all, they have also been filmed and it is now almost impossible to conjure up Long John Silver without thinking of Robert Newton.

However, it is fair to say that Stevenson's short stories are not without their merits; not just tales of diabolic possession like 'Thrawn Janet', or 'Markheim', but also the great stories from his Vailima period. When BBC Radio decided to run a Stevenson short story season in 1991 it was indicative both of RLS's catholicity of output and the drama department's concern for the audience's demands that they balanced two tales from the South Seas with two Edinburgh stories from an earlier period.

I adapted 'The Pavilion on the Links', that aptly melodramatic tale which is so rich in seaside atmosphere remembered from Stevenson's childhood. Given that the sense of place was so pervasive — according to the Tusitala edition 'the scenery was suggested by Dirleton in East Lothian, near North Berwick, and midway between Tantallon and Gillane (sic)' — it seemed to me entirely reasonable to attempt to make the landscape a character in its own right. As the main protagonists play out their tragedy on the links, the breaking of the sea and the moaning of the ever-present wind not only set the scene but frequently intruded on the action. In that way, the coincidences — Cassilis meeting up with Northmour, the immediacy of his love for Clara — make better sense because they were set against a timeless background and were not a part of any 'known' history.

In order to place the story in context, though, I went back to its original version, first published in the Cornhill in 1880, and reintroduced the idea of Cassilis opening the account from his sickbed in old age. Although this is something of a cliché, in radio terms, it worked here, largely because redemption is a central theme and we have to know why Frank Cassilis stands in awe of his tempestuous past.

By its very nature, though, the process of adapting great literature for radio can never be a seamless thing. What reads well on the cold page does not always spring into life on the airwaves. Action has to be speeded up or encapsulated, some characteristics have to be intensified, others muted or even ignored; at all times, the sense of communication has to be paramount even if it means stepping aside from the writer's original intentions. On occasions, the adaptor or producer has to take liberties with the text simply because five minutes of drama, say, can use up five hundred words — just over the length of an average page of text and radio dramas rarely last longer than sixty minutes.

One virtue saves the whole enterprise. Unless the adaptation is written from a solid basis of affection for the original it will never work as a radio production. For that reason, whenever anyone says to me that they heard my play the other night, unless it really is my own — and I have written several — I always reply, 'Not mine but Stevenson's. I just had the pleasure of adapting it.'

And I mean it.

RENNIE McOWAN

WRITES FOR NEWSPAPERS & MAGAZINES ON OUTDOOR THEMES OF HISTORY AND LITERATURE · BOOKS INCLUDE WALKS IN THE TROSSACHS & THE ROB ROY COUNTRY AND THE SCOTTISH SECTION OF ON FOOT THROUGH HISTORY

BORN: 1936 IN ALVA BY THE OCHILS · CHILDREN'S NOVEL LIGHT ON DUMYAT CHOSEN BY CENTRAL REGION FOR THE PRIMARY SCHOOLS CONFERENCE & THE SEQUEL THE WHITE STAG ADVENTURE BROADCAST BY BBC

THE BRECK TREK

THE BRECK TREK

RENNIE McOWAN

Give to me the life I love,
Let the lave go by me,
Give the jolly heaven above
And the byway nigh me...
Wealth I ask not, hope nor love,
Nor a friend to know me;
All I ask, the heaven above
And the road before me.
  SONGS OF TRAVEL

You could blame 'The Sunday Post' for starting it all. When I was a boy they produced *Kidnapped* in picture-strip form and the dramatic drawings captivated me; I still have an evocative look at its well-thumbed pages and it kindled my interest in things Highland and historical.

One of the hills it showed was Uamh Mhor (Var) above the village of Doune and I learned that the Stevenson family had climbed the spectacular peak of Dumyat at the west end of the Ochils. Louis had spent holidays at Bridge of Allan and visited many parts of the Highlands. He had looked at the same view as we Hillfoots people, the great blue wall of the Southern Highlands and the Grampians, the true boundary between Highland and Lowland.

When I was older I too climbed Dumyat and many adult mountaineering expeditions took me to other *Kidnapped* sites; Mull, Morven, Rannoch Moor, Glen Coe, Ben Alder, Balquhidder, Strathyre and I determined to follow the route taken by David Balfour from Earraid to Mull and his meeting with Alan Breck at the wood of Lettermore near Ballachulish, their journeying together over the hills to the Lowlands and thence to Edinburgh.

I proceeded to walk the 'gaps' and discover why Stevenson wrote as he did. Although he did not walk this route he provided an (unreal) map and there is much to puzzle over. I have been doing that for thirty years now.

The precise distance depends on how many diversions are taken and I make the total walking distance around 270 miles of which about 20 are water crossings. I eventually hired boats or got a lift from friends for all the five watercrossings, but in the early days I abandoned the walk on one bank and picked it up again on the other. Modern tarmac roads — which I hate — total about 67 miles and some folk use a bike for them.

There were sometimes gaps of months and years but it was always churning away in my mind. Time too was needed to explore optional routes. There is not space here to give a detailed turn-left-at-the-grey-boulder account, but the flavour of it all remains and the memories linger...

Recuperating on Mull from an illness I seized the chance to wade across to Earraid and then to splash back (in the manner of the 'marooned' David Balfour). I only did it by counting 100 steps at a time because I was very tottery, but I was so elated at knocking off this first stage that I left my camera bag on a rock and the tide got it.

Some folk say one can walk the coastal flats of the Ross of Mull, but this is not on. We tried. Take the obvious line of the historic Glen More pass and walk on the verge, parts of the old road or use a bike.

Patience is needed on the Breck Trek. I made several visits to Torosay Castle, near Craignure, until I found out that the Torosay of Stevenson's day was near Salen. The ferry from Fishnish to Kinlochaline is fun, then comes a long trek across Morven and into Ardgour, a two options section and very rough going. The intricacies of the Appin murder are manifold, sufficient to note that Stevenson switched it from 1752 to 1751. The home of James of the Glen at Acharn is now ruinous but an old stable nearby has become a bothy run by the Mountain Bothies Association. We explored all this on day outings and covered the Glen Coe options in the same way, but some swearing is inevitable with the latter.

Stevenson's map routes the two heroes 'round the back' of the Bidean nam Bian group and then into Glen Coe at a point near Meannarclach, an old goat pen now marked by a heap of stones used as a road block during the Second World War. This — to be frank — does not make sense. The initial route by the rivers Duror and Creran is the obvious way although modern conifer forestry poses problems but it is a very convoluted, tortuous route to get into Glen Coe. We spent two summers and part of one winter on it. The so-called 'Lost Valley' (Coire Gabail) route favoured by some, is bizarre, but the Larig Eilde from Dalness feels right and it is reasonably close to Beinn Maol Chaluim, a hill mentioned by Stevenson by name and which has historic ecclesiastical links.

The blunt truth is that there is no rock and no waterfall in Glen Coe which accurately matches the *Kidnapped* description and the normal claimants, such as Signal Rock, fail on close examination although some have been used in films. My own theory is that Stevenson put a number of sites together including the Falls of Rogie near Strathpeffer, the Bracklinn Falls near Callander and the River Orchy Falls. Nor is it sensible to route the two heroes over the gap between the Pap of Glen Coe and the Aonach Eagach ridge; it is a steep slog but there are attractive woodland paths above modern Glen Coe hospital leading down to Loch Leven.

Stevenson has the two heroes sheltering in a cave near Koalisnacoan clachan, Caolasnacon on modern maps and transformed into a caravan park. A cave can be seen from the shore, high up and just below the Aonach Eagach ridge, and Stevenson may have had that pointed out to him and brought it several hundred feet down the mountainside.

He has been criticised for having dragoons on Rannoch Moor but garrons (Highland ponies) do go on some sections. We made three separate and memorable crossings and it is not clear which way he routed the fugitives to Ben Alder and the

famous Cluny's Cage. We spent two wasted weeks on three
options and might have saved ourselves the trouble since
modern research indicates that the fugitive Cluny MacPherson
had several 'safe houses' and the Cage was probably not on
the spot shown by modern maps. Father David Trainer, of
Glasgow archdiocese, a walking historian, argues persuasively
that the Cage was not on Ben Alder but on the east shore of
Loch Ericht.

The Breck Treck walker must be prepared to walk several
alternative passes, glorious journeys, on his quest. The ruined
MacLaren house of Invernenty to the west of Loch Doine is
the likely site for the famous clan confrontation and piping
scene. A secondary road leads to Strathyre village and then a
cycle track on the old rail line to Callander. For Uamh Mhor
take the road from Callander to a point short of Braeleny
Farm, cross the Keltie Water by a bridge where a forestry road
runs across rough moorland (avoiding hassle for the farmer at
Wester Branklyn). The little cleft where the MacGregors hid
cattle is on the west side of Uamh Mhor and it was probably
Stevenson's interest in that clan that led him to earmark what,
with its bigger neighbour, Uamh Bheag, is otherwise a relatively undistinguished hill. He was also influenced by Scott's
'Lady of the Lake'; the stag starts its journey from the Glen
Artney side of Uamh Mhor.

The descent across moorland to the Allan Water is very
rough (Kippendavie is now called Ryland Lodge) and a charming path from Dunblane to Bridge of Allan passes a cave used
by Stevenson as a boy and which may be the prototype of Ben
Gunn's cave in *Treasure Island*.

A bike is recommended for the road from Stirling to
Limekilns on the Forth. The present inn or 'change house'
which existed in Stevenson's day is not the present inn, but a
renovated dwelling house called Breck House and the wooded headland, where David and Alan hid, can be seen.

The fugitives are rowed across to Carriden (not far from
Bo'ness) and then it is on to Queensferry where the Hawes
Inn is still busy. A charming path leads to Cramond village
and Cramond ferry where Cramond Tower might have been

the prototype for the House of Shaws. Although now demolished, Cammo House has also been suggested.

My patient and long-suffering family posed for photographs on top of Corstorphine Hill near 'Rest and Be Thankful' where Alan and David part for ever.

What has this pastime brought me and my good and helpful friends? Increased respect for Stevenson as a writer, admiration for literary men like the late David Angus and Louis Stott and Captain Ronnie Leask, generous in passing on their knowledge to mountaineers like me, a wider appreciation of the glories of the Highlands and a nagging realisation of how easily so-called wild land can nowadays have the hand of man imprinted on it. Like Stevenson I have 'lovely memories of green days in forest and blue days at sea.' And we're not finished yet —

'There's some good walking in the plot of Catriona!'

LLOYD OSBOURNE

AN INTIMATE
PORTRAIT OF RLS

STEVENSON AT THIRTY-ONE

Davos in 1881 consisted of a small straggling town where nearly all the shops were kept by consumptives. It possessed a charity sanitarium, and three large hotels, widely separated from one another, in which one could die quite comfortably. It was then the 'new Alpine cure' for tuberculosis; and its altitude, its pine woods, and its glorious winter sunshine were supposed to work wonders. For five months of the year — 'the season' — it was buried in snow and rimmed about with daz-

zling white peaks. Snow, snow, snow; icicled trees; a frozen little river; a sense of glinting and sparkling desolation — such
was the place we had come to.

The visitors at the hotels were nearly all English, and though
a considerable proportion of them died, it was amazing what a
gay and animated life they led. The uncertain tenure of life
engendered recklessness even in the staidest. There were wild
love-affairs, tempestuous jealousies, cliques and coteries of the
most belligerent description, and an endless amount of gossip
and back-biting. In our hotel besides, were eleven English
clergymen of every shade of orthodoxy, who made a really
remarkable amount of commotion out of their differences.

The dead were whisked away very unobtrusively. You might
meet Miss Smith coming out of room 46, say — and then suddenly realize that this had been Mrs Robinson's room, and that
you had not seen her for some time. People you had not seen
for some time could usually be found in the cemetery, though
their intervening travels had been marvellously screened from
notice. The only note of tragedy that was ever apparent was at
the weekly weighing of patients. This was done in public, and
one had but to look at the faces to read the verdict of the scales
— consternation in those who were losing; anxiety in the sta-
tionary; an elation that was almost childish amongst the gain-
ers, who would shout out 'two pounds,' or whatever it was,
with offensive triumph in their voices, and oblivious of the bale-
ful glances cast at them.

Fortunately RLS stood the weekly ordeal very creditably.
Davos agreed with him; he steadily gained weight, and was
unquestionably better. My mother and he kept themselves
somewhat aloof from the others, and though friendly and
approachable were never drawn into the passionate enmities
and intimacies of the place. Stevenson was never much at ease
with ordinary, commonplace English people, possibly because
they always regarded him with suspicion. He had untidy hair,
untidy clothes, unconventional convictions, no settled place —
at that time — in the scheme of things; and was moreover married to a *divorcée*. The Hotel Belvedere thought very little of
him, one way or the other, and his only real friend was
Christian, the head waiter, who like many Swiss of mediocre

position, was an extremely intellectual man, with an understanding and outlook far above the average. Together they would pace the empty dining-room for an hour at a time in profound and interminable discussions while the tables were being spread for the next meal.

This was a thoroughly boring and unprofitable winter for Stevenson. His small bedroom was not condusive to work, and he was terribly lacking besides in any incentive. In a sort of desperation he began a novel for my amusement, called 'The Squaw Man', but it never got beyond three chapters. This was the only time in his life when I remember his having anything like mental inertia. It is true he wrote; he was always writing; but fruitlessly, laboriously, and without any sustaining satisfaction. He often had an air of not knowing what to do with himself, and it was in this humor that he often came to my room to join me at play with my tin soldiers, or to interest himself in my mimic enterprises. I had a small printing-press, and used to earn a little money by printing the weekly concert programmes and other trifling commissions; and growing ambitious I became a publisher. My first venture was 'Black Canyon, or Life in the Far West,' a tiny booklet of eight pages, and both the spelling and the matter were entirely original; my second was 'Not I, and Other Poems by R L Stevenson,' price sixpence. How thunderstruck we should have been to know that forty years afterward these were to figure in imposing catalogues as: STEVENSONIANS, EXCESSIVELY RARE, DAVOS PRESS, and be priced at sixty or seventy guineas apiece.

One of the inmates of the hotel was a gaunt, ill-dressed, sallow young woman, the wife of a dying clergyman, who used to waylay me and ask in the most frightening way whether I loved Jesus; and by degrees this embarrassing inquiry was enlarged to include Stevenson, with an urgent desire for information about his spiritual welfare. I tried my best to elude her, but I couldn't. She was always pouncing out of the unlikeliest places to grab my arm before I could escape. Later she made a point descending to the dining-room at the very early and unfrequented hour that Stevenson breakfasted, and started the habit of passing him little notes — all about his soul, and the sleepless nights his spiritual danger was causing her.

Stevenson was as polite and considerate as he was to every one; too polite and considerate, for one morning another breakfaster — a young man who habitually sat near us — detected the transfer of one of these little notes, and that night, swelling with self-righteousness, pointedly ignored Stevenson, and made a stage-play of speaking only to my mother.

This led to an explanation in our bedroom. The young man was sent for, the notes were shown him in the presence of my mother, I gave my childish evidence, and RLS was exonerated. But my principal recollection was his zest in the whole little drama — the unjust accusation, the conspicuous public affront borne in silence, the thumping vindication with its resultant apologies and expressions of regret, and finally the stinging little sermon on scandal and scandal-mongers.

For a month afterward he never went down to breakfast without me; and I was told — vastly to my pride and self-importance — to interpose myself between him and the sallow young lady, and make it impossible for her to slip any more notes into his hand.

STEVENSON AT THIRTY-TWO

Our second winter at Davos was infinitely pleasanter than the first. We were now installed in a *châlet* of our own, with a cook, and plenty of room for all of us. RLS had brought back the half-finished manuscript of *Treasure Island*, begun that summer at Braemar, and with it a revived ardor for work. The *châlet* was bathed in sunshine, and had a delightful outlook over the whole valley; and its seclusion was the more welcome after the crowded hotel, and the enforced intimacy with uncongenial people. RLS seemed to expand in this homelike atmosphere, and his contentment and satisfaction were most apparent.

Before leaving Scotland he had applied for the vacant and highly paid professorship of English literature at Edinburgh University; and full of this new ambition — which had he achieved it would have quickly ended his life in that harsh climate — he gave me a course of trial lectures to see how well he could acquit himself. No wonder that my mother used to smile.

He would walk up and down sonorously addressing the class
— which was I, very self-conscious and uncomfortable — and
roll out with daunting solemnity such phrases as: 'Gentlemen,
before we proceed further I must beg your special attention to
one of the most significant phrases...' 'Gentlemen, before we
can review the condition of England in the year 1337, we
should first envisage the general culture of Europe as a whole.'
'Gentlemen, I hope none of you will make the fatal mistake of
undervaluing the great share, the gigantic share that the
Church, in spite of its defects...'

I was overwhelmed by his commendation.

'I have no fear now,' he said to my mother. 'Lloyd has shown
me that I have the ability to hold a class's attention and interest;
some of it has been over his head, of course, but I can feel that
he has grasped my essential points and has followed me with
quite a remarkable understanding.'

In spite of my pride I felt a dreadful little hypocrite. Except
for the word 'gentlemen,' and some sanguinary details of
medieval life, the lectures had slid off me like water off a duck's
back.

It was about this time I noticed how much darker RLS's hair
was becoming. It had turned to a dark brown, and so lank that
at a little distance it appeared almost black. The hair had a curious way of reflecting one's physical condition; and judging by
this criterion RLS must have been very ill. He no longer tobog-
ganed with me, and seldom walked as far as the town — about
a mile distant. Usually he contented himself with pacing up
and down his veranda, or descending to the foot of our hill to
drop in on John Addington Symonds.

But the influence of such men — academic, and steeped in
the classics — was always subtly harmful to Stevenson, who had
what we would call now an 'inferiority complex' when in contact with them. Their familiarity with the ancient Greeks and
Romans seemed to emphasize his own sense of shortcoming;
made him feel uneducated, and engaged in unimportant tasks;
put him out of conceit with himself and his work. Even as a
boy I could feel the veiled condescension Symonds had for
him.

In his ardor to academize Stevenson, and make him classicly

respectable, he even ferreted out a scarcely known Greek author, and suggested that RLS should collate all the scraps of information about him and write a 'Life.'

All Stevenson's creative work was done in the morning, though in those days before typewriters an author had an interminable amount of writing to do that was merely copying, and involved no mental effort. The writers of to-day never have 'scrivener's cramp,' which pursued RLS all his life, and which caused him often to hold his pen between his second and third fingers when the index-finger was useless. His preference was for white, ruled foolscap paper, chosen because it approximated in his writing to a *Cornhill* page' of five hundred words. His first essays had been taken by the *Cornhill Magazine*, and its page established for him a measure of computation. He calculated the length of all his work in *Cornhill* pages' long after he had ceased all connection with the magazine itself, and indeed as long as he lived.

I think he found rewriting a very soothing pastime, and would not have thanked anybody for a mechanical short cut; it was equivalent, and a much pleasanter one, for the knitting and bead-stringing that doctors nowadays so often enforce on their patients; and it had the agreeable quality that he could pause as long as he liked over a word or a phrase that was not quite to his liking, and polish endlessly. Those who criticise RLS for his excessive particularity are mistaken in their judgement. It was this rewriting and polishing that helped to keep him alive.

But in our second winter in Davos he wrote too little to have much of this aftermath, and was thrown very much on me for the distraction of his afternoons. A more delightful playfellow never lived; my memory of that winter is one of extraordinary entertainment. He engraved blocks and wrote poems for the two tiny books I printed on my press; he painted scenery for my toy theatre — a superb affair, costing upward of twenty pounds and far beyond our purse — that had been given me on the death of the poor lad who had whiled away his dying hours with it at the Belvedere; helped me to give performances and slide the actors in and out on their tin stands, as well as imitating galloping horses, or screaming screams for the heroine in distress. My mother, usually the sole audience, would laugh till she had to be patted on the back, while I held back the play with much impatience for her recovery. But best of all were our 'war games,' which took weeks to play on the attic floor. Stevenson excelled with pistol, while I was a crack shot with the sleeve-link. The leader who first moved his men, no matter how few, into the firing range was entitled to the first shot. If you had thirty regiments you had thirty shots; but your opponent was entitled to as many return shots as he had regiments, regardless of how many you had slaughtered in the meanwhile.

Interesting to know what a love of soldiering RLS always had. Once he told me that if he had had the health he would have gone into the army, and had even made the first start by applying for a commission in the yeomanry — which illness had made him forego.

One conversation I heard him have with a visitor at the *châlet* impressed me irrevocably. The visitor was a fussy, officious person, who after many preambles ventured to criticise Stevenson for the way he was bringing me up. RLS, who was always the most reasonable of men in an argument, and almost over-ready to admit any points against himself, surprised me by his unshaken stand.

'Of course I let him read anything he wants,' he said. 'And if he hears things you say he shouldn't, I am glad of it. A child should early gain some perception of what the world is really like — its baseness, its treacheries, its thinly veneered brutalities; he should learn to judge people and discount human frailty and weakness, and be in some degree prepared and armed for taking his part later in the battle of life. I have no patience with this fairy-tale   training that makes ignorance a virtue. That was how I was brought up, and no one will ever know except myself the bitter misery it cost me.'

Certainly this frankness gave a great charm to our intercourse and a mental stimulation I shall always be grateful for, but some of Stevenson's fancies I absorbed with the soberer facts of life. One in particular was his ineradicable conviction that gold spectacles were the badge of guile. Like Jim Hawkins being warned about the one-legged sea-cook, I was bidden to be watchful of people in gold spectacles. They were deceitful, hypocritical, and flourished on spoliation; they were devoid of all honor and honesty; they went about masked with gold spectacles and apparent benevolence to prey on all they could. I often felt what a good thing it was that they were so plainly marked.

What a story must lie behind this fantasy of Stevenson's! One asks oneself who was this man with the gold spectacles, and what dire part had he played in RLS's past? Perhaps a Lenôtre of some future generation will dig him out his hiding-place and hold him up — gold spectacles and all — to the odium of our descendants.

STEVENSON AT THIRTY-FOUR

When I came out to Hyères in 1884 I had been absent a year from my mother and RLS. A year is an immense period in a growing boy's life, and I was now almost sixteen, with the dawning perceptions of early manhood.

I was aware of a curious change in my family, while in reality the change was largely in myself. I had expected to take up things where I had left off, and felt a little baffled and lonely as I readjusted myself to altered conditions. It was not that RLS was not extremely kind, or that anything was lacking in the warmth of his welcome. But somehow he had receded from me; and though my mother stuffed me with delicacies, and overflowed with confidences about the new life and new interests, she had receded, too. Woggs, the Skye terrier, alone met me on the old basis. That year was nothing to Woggs; there was no recession about *him;* he jumped all over me and smelled the same boy.

This first impression of aloofness gradually disappeared, but on marshalling my recollections it does seem strange that I strolled so seldom with RLS, and talked with him so little, and have nothing of any very personal kind to recall. Perhaps the atmosphere of robust Philistinism I had brought from my English tutor's repelled him; perhaps the effort to turn me into a conventional and commonplace young Englishman had been only too successful. But whatever the explanation, it was at least the only time in my life when Stevenson and I were not delightfully intimate. My own idea is that the routine of his days were so pleasantly filled that I was hardly more than a supernumerary; too old for any childish appeal, and too immature for any other. I was in the nature of an interruption, to be borne with amiably but exciting no special interest.

RLS looked very well, and much better than I last remembered him. His hair was cut short; he wore presentable clothes; and at a little distance, in a straw hat, he might have been mistaken for an ordinary member of society. The short black cape, or *pélerine*, that he always preferred to an overcoat, was a typically French garment, and in France, of course, aroused no comment. In fact I found he had become very much of a Frenchman, even to the little *'Impérial'* on his chin. Speaking French as fluently as his own language; as familiar with French literature and French politics as with English; nowhere more at home than in his adopted country, he had shed nearly everything English about him.

'La Solitude,' as our cottage was called, was a most coquettish little place; it had been exhibited at the World's Fair, and had won the first prize in its class — and looked it. Even the flowers that grew all over it had the unreal quality of stage-setting. Passers-by, gazing up at it from the road below, could be heard commenting on how it had been moved, with every board and brick carefully numbered, from its triumphant exhibition in Paris. It might, indeed, have almost been called one of the sights of Hyères; and the outlook from it, with the islands in the distance, was superb. Here in the midst of a little garden was 'La Solitude,' with the air of asking you to stop for an ice or a souvenir post-card.

It is easy to understand what RLS wrote afterward, that the time he spent in Hyères was the happiest in his life. He was working hard and well; was gaining recognition and making a fair income; had many irons in the fire, or coming out of it: *Prince Otto*, *The Silverado Squatters*, *Penny Whistles* (afterward renamed the *Child's Garden of Verses*), and many essays that were later to become so famous. It is worth noting perhaps that his ambition for Prince Otto was inordinate; some of its chapters he rewrote as many as seven times; of all of his books, save the *Master of Ballantrae* and, later, *Weir*, it was closest to his heart. For the *Child's Garden* on the contrary, which will probably outlive all his work and has entered into the soul of the race, his attitude was more of an indulgent indifference once the poems had been collected. I remember his saying: 'By Jove, I believe I could make a little book out of those things if I wrote a few more; they are trifling enough, but not without a certain charm.'

The routine of his existence suited him to perfection — at his desk all the morning; then luncheon, with an excellent *vin du pays*, and never lacking a salad; a stroll afterward in the sunshine, to drop in and talk politics with old Le Roux, the wine-merchant, or to have a chat with his friend Powell, the English chemist. Then home to look over his correspondence and write a few letters, with an excellent little dinner to follow and a conversation shared by Valentine, our vivacious cook and maid of all work. She was a charming girl, far above her class, and with a sparkling sense of humor, who reviewed the whole neighborhood and nightly brought its annals up to date.

Although RLS always wrote so feelingly about his friends it was remarkable how well he could do without them. Few men had so little need of intimacies as he. Human intercourse of some kind was essential; it was the breath of life to him; but any one with any originality of mind and power of expression would suffice. RLS loved talk and argument and discussion; it refreshed him; exhilarated him; brought him home with brightened eyes and a good appetite. It was his form of cocktail.

It must be remembered that he was one of the most prepossessed men that ever lived. Call him an egoist if you like; such is the common reproach of his critics; but it was his work that always came first, that animated all his thoughts, that was the consuming joy and passion of his life. Unconsciously I think he graded his friends by their interest in it; regraded them as helpful satellites who could assist and cheer him on his way. Doubtless this statement will be thought cynical — almost a disparagement. But it is neither. Stevenson offers the fascinating study of a man whose spiritual concentration kept him alive. He simply wouldn't die; refused to; and those who would have him different would not now be reading his books — because there would have been no books. In the light of modern psychology it is very plain what enabled him to hold death at bay till forty-four, while so many of his generation with the same disease, and infinitely less impaired, succumbed long before him. First, it was this tremendous prepossession for his work, and secondly his invincible refusal to become an invalid. He was never willing to coddle himself, or to acquiesce in illness if he could possibly avoid doing so. He would say, with his habitual emphasis and determination: 'Oh, hell, what does it matter? Let me die with my boots on.'

It has always been a satisfaction to me that he did. Unlacing them as he lay dead, that reiterated remark of his came back to me very poignantly. Intrepid to the end, he had had his wish, which was symbolic of so much more.

I often think it was a mistake he ever left Hyères; it was so entirely congenial and suited him so well, though the last word must be used in a relative sense. The reason was absurd. My mother, with a view of keeping up with the advance of medicine and gaining some things that might help RLS, subscribed to the *Lancet* — the well known medical weekly. It was the worst reading in the world for her, as it is for any layman who foolishly tries to trespass on a highly technical domain. Stevenson, true to himself and wiser, left it severely alone. But my mother glued herself to it, and began to fill her mind with all sorts of bogeys. Vinegar was discovered to be full of perils; salads carried the eggs of tapeworms; salt hardened your arteries and shortened your days; heaven only knows what all she discovered in the way of lurking dangers, previously undreamed of; and when the climax came in an outbreak of cholera in the old part of the town, with a terrible death-roll amongst its poor, dirty, neglected inhabitants, she fell into a panic and began to work on RLS to abandon Hyères as a place too dangerous to live in.

Had it not been for the *Lancet*, I doubt if RLS would ever have left Hyères.

STEVENSON AT THIRTY-FIVE

Wensleydale was one of a tall row of lodging-houses on the West Cliff of Bournemouth, overlooking the sands below, and with a gloriously sparkling view of the Needles and the Isle of Wight. In that Golden Age there was a whole race of people who kept such houses, and who made you extremely comfortable and often fed you admirably for a few shillings a week.

It was lovely autumn weather when RLS and my mother arrived. They were in the highest of spirits; everything pleased them; and although they were carrying all they possessed with them, and had neither home nor plans — and ought to have been rather forlorn, one should think — they were as happy as grigs, and seemed not to have a care in the world. They were supposed to come for a few weeks to see a little of me before I left my tutor's to enter Edinburgh University; nothing was further from their minds than to remain in England; it was taken for granted that they would finally return to the Continent to seek another and a more hygienic Hyères. Little could they foresee that their visit to Bournemouth was destined to last almost three years; and was then to lead, not to France or Italy but to America and the South Sea Islands.

I am dwelling on the gaiety of those months at 'Wensleydale' because it marked what might be called the end of an epoch in Stevenson's life. He was never afterward so boyish or so light-hearted; it was the final flare-up of his departing youth. The years that followed, however full they were of interest and achievement, were grayer; it was a soberer and a more preoccupied man that lived them. The happy-go-lucky Bohemian who had been rich if he could jingle ten pounds in his pocket, and who talked so cheerfully of touring France in a caravan, giving patriotic lectures with a magic lantern on 'The Incomparable Colonies of France' — with an ensuing collection in the lecturer's hat — was soon to discover that success had its penalties as well as its sweets. It was all inevitable of course; such hard work could not escape its reward, and none of us can keep back the clock. Stevenson is to be envied that he retained his youth as long as he did. But he left it at 'Wensleydale.'

Henley came — a great, glowing massive-shouldered fellow with a big red beard and a crutch; jovial, astoundingly clever, and with a laugh that rolled out like music. Never was there such another as William Ernest Henley; he had an unimaginable fire and vitality; he swept one off one's feet. There are no words that can describe the quality he had of exalting those about him; he was the first man I had ever called by his surname; the first friend I had ever sought and won; he said the most flattering things of me behind my back, and intoxicated me by his regard. How I idolized him!

And he had come to make us all rich! Yes, the secret of Crœsus was in that shabby little black writing-case. We were enveloped in a gorgeous dream; the dingy walls of 'Wensleydale' receded, and we found ourselves in a palace of 'The Arabian Nights': Dreams, dreams, and always the cadence of that unforgotten voice!

RLS was no longer to plod along as he had been doing; Henley was to abandon his grinding and ill-paid editorship; together they would combine to write plays — marvellous plays that would run for hundreds of nights and bring in thousands of pounds.

RLS entered enthusiastically into this collaboration, though with his underlying Scotch caution I doubt if he allowed himself to be wholly transported into Henley's fairy-land. But he was stirred, nevertheless; shared to some degree, though reservedly, those ardent day-dreams of wealth; worked at the plays with extraordinary gusto and industry. *Beau Austin* was written in four days, and I shall never forget Henley reading it aloud — so movingly, so tenderly that my eyes were wet with tears. But deep down within me was a disappointment I tried hard to stifle.

But disillusionment was slow in coming, even though the succeeding plays pleased me as little as the first. The gorgeous dream was not so easily wafted away. It persisted — for me at least — long after we had left that fairy palace on the West Cliff. But Stevenson, I think, came soonest out of the spell — was the first to rub his eyes and recover his common sense. His ardor certainly declined; in the interval of Henley's absences he very gladly returned to his own work, and had as a playwright to be resuscitated by his unshaken collaborator, who was as confident and eager as ever.

RLS lost not only the last flicker of his youth in 'Wensleydale,' but I believe also any conviction that he might become a popular dramatist.

STEVENSON AT THIRTY-SEVEN

Skerryvore was an unusually attractive suburban house, set in an acre and a half of ground; and its previous owner — a retired naval captain — had been at no little expense to improve and add to it. Somehow it was typical of an old sailor; it was so trim, so well arranged, so much thought had been given to its many conveniences.

The house and five hundred pounds toward furnishing it were a wedding present to my mother from RLS's parents. The wanderers were now anchored; over their heads was their own roof-tree; they paid rates and taxes, and were called on by the vicar; Stevenson, in the word he hated most of all, had become the 'burgess' of his former jeers. Respectability, dullness, and similar villas encompassed him for miles in every direction.

In his heart I doubt if he really ever liked 'Skerryvore'; he never spoke of it with regret; left it with no apparent pang. The Victorianism it exemplified was jarring to every feeling he possessed, though with his habitual philosophy he not only endured it, but even persuaded himself that he liked it. But so far as he had any snobbishness it was his conviction — which was really somewhat naîve — that artists were instinctive aristocrats, who never could be content in the middle class. I suppose when he said 'artists' he meant himself, and certainly of all men he was the least fitted for ordinary English suburban life. Not that he saw much of it. He was virtually a prisoner in that house the whole time he lived in it; for him those years in 'Skerryvore' were gray, indeed.

His health throughout was at its lowest ebb; never was he so spectral, so emaciated, so unkempt and tragic a figure. His long hair, his eyes, so abnormally brilliant in his wasted face, his sick-room garb, picked up at random and to which he gave no thought — all are ineffaceably pictured in my mind; and with the picture is an ineffable pity. Once at sunset I remember him entering the dining-room, and with his cloak already about him, mutely interrogating my mother for permission to stroll in the garden. It had rained for several days and this was his first opportunity for a breath of outside air.

'Oh, Louis, you mustn't get your feet wet,' she said in an imploring voice.

He made no protest; he was prepared for the denial. But such a look of despair crossed his face that it remains with me yet. Then still silent he glanced again toward the lawn with an inexpressible longing. Afterward in Samoa I reminded him of that little scene at a moment when his exile was weighing most heavily on him. We were both on horseback and had stopped for a cigarette; the palms were rustling in the breeze, and the lovely shores of Upolu far below were spread out before us in the setting sun. He gave a little shudder at the recollection I had evoked, and after a moody pause exclaimed: 'And all for five minutes in a damned back yard! No, no no, I would be a fool ever to leave Samoa!' And, as though to emphasize the contrast, dug the spurs into his horse and started off at a headlong gallop.

Of course his health varied. There were periods when he was comparatively well when he would go to London to spend a few days. Once he even got as far as Paris; once he went to Dorchester to see Thomas Hardy, and continuing on to Exeter was overtaken by an illness that lasted three weeks and brought him to death's door. But in general he was a prisoner in his own house and saw nothing of Bournemouth save his own little garden. There could be no pretence he was not an invalid and a very sick man. He had horrifying haemorrhages, long spells when he was doomed to lie motionless on his bed lest the slightest movement should restart the flow, when he would speak in whispers, and one sat beside him and tried to be entertaining — in that room he was only too likely to leave in his coffin.

How thus handicapped he wrote his books is one of the marvels of literature — books so robustly and aboundingly alive that it is incredible they come out of a sick-room; and such well-sustained books with no slowing down of their original impetus, nor the least suggestion of those intermissions when their author lay at the point of death. Those years in 'Skerryvore' were exceedingly productive. The *Strange Case of Dr Jekyll and Mr Hyde* was written; so was *Kidnapped;* so was *Markheim,* and any number of his best short stories; so too, was the *Life of Fleeming Jenkin*. One day he came down to luncheon in a very preoccupied frame of mind, hurried through his meal — an unheard of thing for him to do — and on leaving said he was working with extraordinary success on a new story that had come to him in a dream, and that he was not to be interrupted or disturbed even if the house caught fire.

For three days a sort of hush descended on 'Skerryvore'; we all went about, servants and everybody, in a tiptoeing silence; passing Stevenson's door I would see him sitting up in bed filling page after page, and apparently never pausing for a moment. At the end of three days the mysterious task was finished and he read aloud to my mother and myself the first draft of *Strange Case of Dr Jekyll and Mr Hyde*.

I listened to it spellbound. Stevenson, who had a voice the greatest actor might have envied, read it with an intensity that made shivers run up and down my spine. When he came to the end, gazing at us in triumphant expectancy and keyed to a pitch of indescribable self-satisfaction — as he waited, and I waited, for my mother's outburst of enthusiasm — I was thunderstruck at her backwardness. Her praise was constrained; the words seemed to come with difficulty; and then all at once she broke out with criticism. He had missed the point, she said; had missed the allegory; had made it merely a story — a magnificent bit of sensationalism — when it should have been a masterpiece.

Stevenson was beside himself with anger. He trembled; his hand shook on the manuscript; he was intolerably chagrined. His voice, bitter and challenging, overrode my mother's in a fury of resentment. Never had I seen him so impassioned, so outraged, and the scene became so painful that I went away, unable to bear it any longer. It was with a sense of tragedy that I listened to their voices from the adjoining room, the words lost but fraught with an emotion that struck at my heart.

When I came back my mother was alone. She was sitting, pale and desolate before the fire, and staring into it. Neither of us spoke. Had I done so it would have been to reproach her, for I thought she had been cruelly wrong. Then we heard Louis descending the stairs, and we both quailed as he burst in as though to continue the argument even more violently than before. But all he said was: 'You are right! I have absolutely missed the allegory, which after all, is the whole point of it — the very essence of it.' And with that, as though enjoying my mother's discomfiture and her ineffectual start to prevent him, he threw the manuscript into the fire! Imagine my feelings — my mother's feelings — as we saw it blazing up; as we saw those precious pages wrinkling and blackening and turning into flame!

My first impression was that he had done it out of pique. But it was not. He really had been convinced, and this was his dramatic amend. When my mother and I both cried out at the folly of destroying the manuscript he justified himself vehemently. 'It was all wrong,' he said. 'In trying to save some of it I should have got hopelessly off the track. The only way was to put temptation beyond my reach.'

Then ensued another three days of feverish industry on his part, and of a hushed anxious, and tiptoeing anticipation on ours; of meals where he scarcely spoke; of evenings unenlivened by his presence; of awed glimpses of him, sitting up in bed, writing, writing, writing, with the counterpane littered with his sheets. The culmination was *Jekyll and Hyde*.

The writing of it was an astounding feat from whatever aspect it may be regarded. Sixty-four thousand words in six days; more than ten thousand words a day. To those who know little of such things I may explain that a thousand word a day is a fair average for any writer of fiction. Anthony Trollope set himself this quota; it was Jack London's; it is — and has been — a sort of standard of daily literary accomplishment. Stevenson multiplied it by ten; and on top of that copied out the whole in another two days and had it in the post on the third!

It was a stupendous achievement; and the strange thing was that, instead of showing lassitude afterward, he seemed positively refreshed and revitalized; went about with a happy air; was as uplifted as though he had come into a fortune; looked better than he had in months.

When I abandoned college at the end of my second year, and returned to 'Skerryvore' with the intention of becoming an author myself under RLS's tuition, I was dismayed to find that he had become religious. Not in the ordinary sense, but as a sort of disciple of Tolstoy's, then at the crest of his fame. Christianity without Christ — that was about what it amounted to — and RLS expatiated on it at great length, and with an air of intense earnestness.

To a young collegian, fresh from an austere and uncongenial Scottish household, where the playing-cards were hidden when the minister called, and Sunday was almost entirely spent at church, it was disconcerting to the last degree to find his home thus altered for the worse. My beloved Louis, one of the most fiery of men, whose very mien as he once raised a row about a corked bottle of wine had emptied half a restaurant — to see him thus reduced to a turning-the-other-cheek condition was nothing less than appalling. I wrestled with him as best I could, but ineffectually. Tolstoyism had always its mild but persistent answer, which after all was rather irrefutable: 'Do nothing to increase the area of suffering, and in time all suffering will disappear.'

RLS was then steeped, not only in Tolstoy, but in all modern Russian literature. Perhaps its sombre and hopeless life suited his own sombre and hopeless life. One of the most dramatic of men, perhaps he here sought and discovered a striking rôle that he himself could fill despite his ill health and imprisoned existence. But be that as it may, a nightmarish plan began to take shape in his mind, and one so typically Russian that I think it must have sprung from this source. To explain it more fully I must digress a little. He had been much worked up over the lawless state of Ireland, which was then filling the English press with revolting stories of boycotts and oppressions — people starving in the midst of plenty, their money refused at every shop; widows sitting beside dead husbands whom none would bury; cattle hamstrung; men struck down; women stripped and flogged; a most dreadful persecution of those who dared rent farms from which the previous tenants had been evicted by the British Government.

RLS's plan though nightmarish was quite simple. We were all to go to Ireland, rent one of these farms, and be murdered in due course. As RLS expressed it with an oratorical flourish: 'The murder of a distinguished English literary man and his family, thus engaged in the assertion of human rights, will arrest the horror of the whole civilized world and bring down its odium on these miscreants.'

Such was the formula of practical Tolstoyism which, though it sounds incredibly absurd, RLS had the most serious intention of carrying out. Indeed, he was in the deadliest earnest, and my mother scarcely less so, unbelievable as it then seemed to me. I suspect, nevertheless, that she would have thwarted the project had it ever matured into action; looking back on it I remember she was much more calm than the circumstances warranted. But to all appearances I was the chief martyr in this Irish fantasy, I, who cared nothing about evicted farmers, nor 'areas of suffering,' nor figuring in a Russian romance ending in the death of a whole family of whom I was one. I wanted to learn to write.

Then RLS's father died suddenly, and we all had to go to Edinburgh to attend the funeral. I returned soon after, but my mother and RLS remained several weeks. In the course of time two letters arrived, the first from my mother — such a heart-broken letter — saying that the doctors had ordered RLS to leave England at once for Colorado as the only means of pro-longing his life. England was ended for him; he was never to set foot in it again. She wrote of her 'little nest' and unen-durable wrench it would be to leave it. 'Life had been too happy in Skerryvore — the envying gods had struck it down.' It was all in this strain of anguish at abandoning her home for a future that loomed before her black indeed.

Expecting to find RLS's in a similar note of tragedy, I opened it — when it arrived a day or two later — with a sinking heart. But it was cheerful, almost jubilant; the prospect of Colorado or New Mexico seemed to fill him with joy. Were we not to live in the wilds with rifles on our walls and bearskins on our mud floors! Sombreros, ha, ha! Mustangs, silver spurs, spacious-ness, picturesque freedom; 'Scottie' of the something or other ranch! There was not a word about cosy nests, nor envying gods, nor eternal farewells to happiness. None whatever. '*Vive la vie sauvage!*' He was plainly glad to be off, and the sooner the better. When at last he did return to 'Skerryvore' it was in the same spirit of elation.

One might have thought that this was the ideal moment to go

to Ireland; why Colorado and an uncertain search for health when in three weeks the whole matter could be so easily and definitely settled by bullets in our backs?

I have often wondered since whether the Irish venture had not its origin in an unsuspected desire to leave 'Skerryvore' at any price. Hopelessly embedded there, locked in and double-locked, had he not seized on this as the one possible means of escape?

PART IV

THE WANDERER
"LOUIS"

HUNTER DAVIES

BROADCASTER FOR BBC RADIO 4 · JOURNALIST WITH PROFILES IN YOU MAGAZINE AND THE INDEPENDENT · MARRIED TO NOVELIST MARGARET FORSTER, THEY LIVE IN LONDON/LAKE DISTRICT · TELLER OF TALES — IN SEARCH OF RLS PUBLISHED 1994

BORN: 1936, RENFREWSHIRE · GREW UP IN CARLISLE · BA. (DUNELM) · BOOKS INCLUDE BIOGRAPHIES OF THE BEATLES, GEORGE STEPHENSON, WILLIAM WORDSWORTH, COLUMBUS, PLUS NOVELS, TRAVEL BOOKS, CHILDRENS' FICTION

"DEAR LOUIS,.."

"DEAR LOUIS..."
HUNTER DAVIES

But we are all travellers in what John Bunyan calls the wilderness of this world all, too, travellers with a donkey; and the best that we find in our travels is an honest friend. He is a fortunate voyager who finds many. We travel, indeed to find them. They are the end and the reward of life. They keep us worthy of ourselves; and when we are alone, we are only nearer to the absent.
TRAVELS WITH A DONKEY

If I may be so bold. Louis, looks funny, though not as funny as it sounds, having to pronounce the s at the end, as your friends did, and the French never do.. Visually, Lewis would suit better, and be much more Scottish, and of course be correct, as it was your birth name. A mite pretentious, I always think, adopting the French spelling when you were 18, but you were a bit of a poseur, trying to cut an artistic dash. I suspect you tried on Louis for size when you picked up your first velvet jacket and thought hmm, quite a neat fit, I'll wear both of these from now on.

These last two years, during which I've been thinking of you every day, you are always RLS. Rarely Stevenson, though I know this was how your oldest male friends addressed you, in the style of your times. I never think of you as Louis. But as Dear Fanny always called you that, and your mother, and presumably a few other familial intimates, I have decided that's how I'll talk to you. It is our style, in this present and very strange world, to address every person by their Christian name, whether you have met them before or not. So, here goes, my dear Louis, my first letter to you.

More a progress report, really, bits and pieces falling from my mind, from my notebook, from my journeys, landing on the page at random, the sort of things I would love to tell you, fact to face, hoping they would amuse, spark off your own memories. For I have set myself the task of following your footsteps. Not exactly an original idea, as you will doubtless say. I imagine you have been watching from the top of Mt. Vaea the various happenings enacted in your name these last 100 years. Do they send free books, to the Great Library in the Sky? As the British Museum gets a copy of every book printed, I think it would — should — be a law that every person biographied should get a copy, whether living or dead.

I've just been across to my RLS bookshelves, 200 books by or about you collected so far. Does that surprise you, including, hold on, I'll just count, 12 first editions? Good, hmm. They tend, alas, to be the later books, when first editions of your works were being printed by the barrow load. I still haven't got first editions of the early ones, such as *An Inland Voyage*. I like that better by the way than *Travels with a Donkey*, which is still the better known of the two, as it was in your time. Funny how constant the public are. My own theory is that the second title was better, and the subject matter. Belgian canals sound awfully dreary. Travels with a donkey in France is a brilliant idea. Environmentally and ecologically very sound. Right on, Louis. (I'll explain why these things matter another day, when I have more time.)

I have just taken down a book from my library published in 1903 called 'Stevenson's Shrine' by some old biddy* who had gone on a pilgrimage to Samoa. I wonder if she was the first. Good photos. Ah, now over here is that brilliant special edition of the 'Bookman' for 1913, in which they had lots of writers and old friends, writing about the various places associated with you. I've also got a 1915 copy of 'On the Trail of Stevenson' by Clayton Hamilton, an American, I suspect, published by Doubleday. He would appear to be the first to attempt what I am trying to do — which is one person following all your footsteps. Mine, however, will be more personal. One chapter will be the past, telling your biography, while the next will be me today, arriving in the same place, describing

* Laura Stubbs!

what I find and what happens to me. So, the reader will get two books for the price of one. In the biographical bits I will try to end each chapter at a good bit, an exciting point, so readers will be desperate for the next chapter. What do you think of the idea? I've used this device several times in books. Well, it amuses me. I have this self imposed rule of never jumping ahead, never referring or disclosing facts yet to come. I hate biographies where they jump ahead and tell you about children, when the person is not even married, or their famous books, when he or she has not written one yet. I've written about the same number of books as you by the way, and they cover a similar range — travel, fiction, children's books, biographies — but there the similarities end. I am a mere hack, my dear friend, a word shifter.

I like to think that physically we are not too unalike. I have similar moustache, dark hair, thin face, not quite as thin else-where as I was, alas. I plan to slim for publication day. Probably get a velvet jacket, and push my Scottishness. I was born in Renfrewshire, of pure Scottish parents, but we moved over the border to Carlisle when I was eleven. I have another two years* of pleasure and exploration to go, and have not yet been to California or to Samoa, two big trips I am saving for later this year. Samoa, by the way, is almost as hard to get to as it was in your day. California, now, no problem, flights almost on the hour, round the clock. You must know what flights are. You were always fascinated by new inventions, such as typewriters and cameras, but I sense you would not have liked aeroplanes. You were too much in love with boats, especially sailing boats, something I find hard to understand. Endless boredom, plus sickness. I think you liked the image of yourself, fearless against the elements, communing with nature, persuading yourself you were having a spiritual as well as physical adventure.

EDINBURGH — I have visited umpteen times in the course of the book and Louis, dear Louis, you would love to go back to Heriot Row. The house is very much as your mother had it,

* (written in Spring 1992)

so I like to imagine, though some of the top floor rooms have changed in shape over the years. I had the honour of sleeping there one night, in the bedroom your parents used, and I like to think I heard the same noises, saw the same views, perhaps experienced the same sensations as you. Heriot Row and the gardens opposite have not changed. Still very select.

No museum devoted solely to your good self, alas. You have to share Lady Stair's House with Burns and Scott. You are in the basement, no don't get hiffy, the presentation is good and the letters and memorabilia most interesting. What would really amuse you is the big plaque in St Giles Cathedral. Remember that one done of you in New York by that chap whose name escapes me?* I have it on a disc but I use a cheap Amstrad word processor and it takes me ages to exit and enter and all that stuff — oh sorry, you won't understand any of this. Neither do I, really. Anyway, on the original plaque you are stretched out, as was your wont, writing away, holding a cigarette. In the St Giles version you are holding a pen. They deemed it more suitable and more kirk-like.

THE CEVENNES — I recently travelled in the Cevennes, but mostly with a Ford Escort — don't tell my publisher. (He's Scottish originally, Sinclair Stevenson, but not one of your branches). I did hire a donkey at Monastier from a local farmer, but gave up after a day as it was too slow. You are not popular, by the way, with local farmers hiring out donkeys. You are alleged to have been cruel, beating your donkey, through your own ignorance, not using the right ropes and not realising when Modestine, your female donkey, was on heat. In Monastier I tracked down the grand-daughter of your landlady, the one you stayed with. I have her name on file, no time to get it now, but I'll describe her house another time to you. Why did you go, by the way? Yes, I know it was to get over Fanny leaving, and you wanted to do a book, I know all that. But why that particular route? I haven't found out who recommended it to you. I feel sure someone did. If so, I don't think much of their advice. Until you actually get to the

* (Augustus St Gaudens)

Cevennes, which is only the last bit of your journey, the landscape is very dour, grim, and barren. Monastier is still a bit of
a dump. Nowhere to eat, nowhere to stay.

HYÉRES — Now that is pretty. You chose well there, old
friend. You didn't point out that Old Hyéres, the ancient part
of the town around the chateau, is actually very like the Old
Town in Edinburgh. The thought struck me at once. Much
smaller of course, lower buildings. It's still very attractive,
well preserved, clean and proper, full of flower boxes. The
tourists and visitors these days all stick to the coast itself and
hardly venture inland. Your house is still there and I had
good fun with the present occupant. I thought he was going
to thump me at first, rushing out in a leather jacket and a
shaven head, all angry because I'd upset his frightening guard-
dog. I picked up a good photo when I was there, which I
have not seen before. It shows La Solitude in your day — but
with a little bridge going from it, across the road. Why did
you never mention that?

You'll be pleased to know that in the tourist office they have
up on the wall that famous remark of yours, translated into
French of course, saying that in Hyéres you were the happiest
you'd ever been. Now I've been there, I can see why you
liked it. I can appreciate why you were happy there — in the
first flush of married life, just you and Fanny, and the books
starting to do well. What I can't understand is why you
weren't as happy, if not happier, later? Were not any of those
years in Samoa as good as Hyéres?

BOURNEMOUTH — Not a lot to see there, and I don't
know how you will take this. A bomb destroyed Skerryvore in
the last war. Yup, all gone. Sorry. But don't fret, they have
got the foundations laid out, tracing the house's shape, plus
the garden leading down to the Chimes, and it is now a little
public garden, with roses and chairs and a model of the
Stevenson lighthouse; very quiet, very peaceful. The street
opposite is called Robert Louis Stevenson Avenue. I walked
down to the beach from your house, and to my surprise, I
could see the Scottish connections, which must have attracted

you. All those pine trees. Very Highlandy.

I live in London myself, which you knew very well, and you are not forgotten here. Near me, across in Hampstead, there is a house in Mount Vernon called Abernethy House, so that sounds Scottish, which has a large plaque outside saying 'Robert Louis Stevenson, 1850-94, Lived Here.' Bit of a liberty, if you ask me, inferring you lived your whole life there. I can't find a reference to it in your letters, but presumably you visited old Sidney Colvin there. Please advise, if you have time to drop me a note. In the meantime, I'll send you another letter when I get back from Samoa. Can't wait.

I am, yours gratefully,
Hunter Davies.

Elizabeth Stuart Warfel

BORN: PHILIPPINES, EDUCATION: SAN FRANCISCO & NEW YORK · INTERIOR DESIGNER · ORGANISER OF THE CARRIAGE TRADE & VICTORIA STREET DESIGNS BETWEEN USA & SCOTLAND

STAGE CAREER AS SOLOIST WITH BALLET COMPANIES IN UK, SWEDEN & USA · LECTURER, WRITER & RADIO WORK · MARRIED WITH 3 CHILDREN & LIVES IN CALIFORNIA

Happier for His Presence (II)

HAPPIER FOR HIS PRESENCE (II)

ELIZABETH STUART WARFEL

The future is nothing; but the past is myself, my own history, the seed of my present thoughts, the mould of my present disposition. It is not in vain that I return to the nothings of my childhood; for every one of them has left some stamp upon me or put some fetter on my boasted free-will. In the past is my present fate; and in the past also is my real life.

A RETROSPECT

Robert Louis Stevenson and I met sixteen years ago in Monterey, California at the old French Hotel, now the Stevenson House. Our eyes connected, his from photographs on the walls; and in dusty showcases, peering from behind lank strands of hair; out from faded images of past adventures. Eyes that above all told you *he* knew something special about you, something you barely knew yourself. Eyes that implored you to think: Why am I here? What am I doing with this life? Have I really fulfilled my greatest potential? Am I marking time? Hiding? Who were you they questioned 'sound of body and I thank you of mind' to be wasting your life. So much fun to be had, roaring adventures and just by the way (as if it were a mere bagatelle) growth, insight and love. The adventure was all, those eyes said — the courage to put the hand in the dark, the insight would come along to the child passenger on the train situated behind the great steam engine chugging and snorting its way along the track. Along, this wisdom, along for the ride. It was small and innocent, delighted by the sights unfolding, this most precious object, this child-seer.

To get up and out and on the track in the first place, this was all.

I do not think I ever quite forgave my American mother for taking me away from my father's country and, just when all the fun was beginning, leaving Scotland. To a small child the excitement among the adults was electrifying... gas masks (your very own in a small brown burlap case), air raid drills, then eventually the real thing: self importance at dusk as you ran around the house securing the thick shiny black cloth to the windows; extended bedtimes, evacuee playmates from the inner city. I prayed for it to never end. I was at the centre of this new experience and my mother was about to spoil it all and run away. It was running away, I could see it in the eyes of the neighbours even if she couldn't — were we cowards? Was that it? Or, as she said: 'We didn't want to get caught up in Europe with Daddy so far away in the Philippines.'

My protestations notwithstanding, we left in early September. Mother qualified for 'US citizen stranded in Europe' status. I however did not, and patriot that I was, held secret hopes that my nationality would, at the very least, delay our departure. A compromise was finally reached and I was assigned a pallet on the floor so that no American was denied his, or her, inalienable right to rescue.

Sorely pressed for war news in those early 'phoney war' days our arrival in Hoboken was given front page centre head-lines:

'Toy sub from U-boat zone.' Underneath, a now fast-fading photo of a sombre nine year old descending the gang plank, baby doll tightly clutched in one arm, in the other a crude 'shipboard-made' wooden submarine with a tenpenny nail conning tower. All that today remains of a journey from the Broomielaw, past Sandy Hook, down the Clyde with California, by train, the final destination.

Such a journey had also been made by Roberet Louis Stevenson some sixty years before. It changed the course of his life, and it changed the course of mine.

In Scotland, Stevenson had been part of my childhood, as he was with children all over the world. A *Child's Garden of*

Verses were read to me and the lovely cadence of the poetry easy to repeat and without any real effort committed to memory. My own 'Leerie' was watched at teatime in the winter dusk when he lighted the lamps outside our surburban Glasgow home in those long-gone pre-war days.

It was summer however that stands out in memory now. Magic moments just before midnight when Mother usually mowed the lawn that stretched from the front door, in a lovely arc to the street below.

'Catch the last bit of light,' she would say and I followed her out unnoticed, to roll about in the newly cut mounds of grass, squeezing the damp smell into my soul.

I have to go to bed by day — 'to have to go to bed by day,' Not me, lucky me. Weren't Scottish summers wonderful? Poor little boy whose nanny packed him off to bed by day, to hear the footsteps on the street when it stayed light so late at night.

Being an only child I somehow felt the little 'Child's Garden boy' with a papa rich as he could be and I were brother and sister and what is more, he understood and cared.

Years later, talking to a teacher in Ayrshire about teaching Stevenson to her young pupils, she expressed the idea that children take him to themselves and eventually leave you out. It's a secretive thing and they seem surprised at the end of the year that you existed at all in the equation. Somehow childhood and childhood alone is the bond.

(Or the child in all of us!)

In America I eventually lost my accent but not my memories or love of Scotland. My Scottish father returned from the Philippines just in time, as it turned out, to experience from afar the agony of Pearl Harbour and his friends and neighbours imprisoned en masse, at Santo Tomas in Manila. Declared an alien by the US government he went to Canada to work out his feelings of guilt and frustration at the shipyards in Vancouver. After the war he returned to the Philippines as head of the British Ministry of War Transport to sort out the tangle of British merchant shipping left behind in Manila and then back to Britain.

I was finally granted my wish to come home. It was easy to

transfer my ballet studies from Balanchine's School of American Ballet in New York to the back streets of Soho in London. Eventually I found myself cast as the Crystal Fairy for sixteen weeks at the Theatre Royal in Glasgow. However it was not this early theatrical engagement that completed for me the emotional circle back to Scotland. It was when Stevenson came back into my life after I entered the French Hotel in Monterey that I began to understand a part of myself long dormant. I remet the Scottish *'Child's Garden'* boy of my childhood and I was hooked.

In the years that followed I read everything on and by RLS. One thing became clear. Nobody seemed to know nor especially care for the writings of the Stevenson that was emerging. Fun-loving, magic, revealing letter-writer, philosopher; way ahead of his time he had somehow become 'out of fashion', relegated to merely a writer of children's stories, albeit good ones. He had for others, like myself, ceased to exist for the adult reader. Somehow, I resolved to be part of a resurgence of interest in Stevenson the man and his works. It seemed presumptious as I thought of it, impossible, and why me... and how?

It is London, time: the present. All the contributors are in and the work finished, we carried the embryo book down the long pink hall and up the stairs to the publisher's office. I somehow felt flat. The quest was over that had taken me from California to Edinburgh to open a shop on Victoria Street where, among the wallpapers and fabrics, I also pursued my interest in Stevenson. The shop was now closed and my permanent link with Scotland broken, I was to return only periodically to the cottage in East Lothian.

It had been an amazing period from which a sense of self began to emerge. The pure essence of Stevenson as he would have wanted it to be? Experiencing the love of the city yet at the same time knowing something of its misery. Stevenson had shared with us some of the problems of his life in his native Edinburgh; in some respect times have changed little. The job was to tackle something impossibly difficult and be alive in the attempt, keep a sense of perspective and humour and somehow, if possible, persevere all the while.

'Acts may be forgiven; not even God can forgive the hanger-back.'

In Edinburgh I had become aware of an odd transformation, almost addiction, in many friends once they were introduced to Stevenson. Often they laughed when we talked about it, having noticed it themselves, as if this were some sort of slight affliction.

There was also an intriguing aspect of RLS emerging. Perhaps I was just imagining it, living with history all around and being so much a part of the fabric of the old city. Whatever it was, I felt an unseen force at work as Stevenson himself had felt his 'little people' his 'Brownies', nudging and prodding, even writing for him.

> Who are the Little People? They are near connections of the dreamer's, beyond doubt; they share in his financial worries and have an eye to the bank-book; they share plainly in his training; they have plainly learned like him to build the scheme of a considerate story and to arrange emotion in progressive order; only I think they have more talent; and one thing is beyond doubt, they can tell him a story piece by piece, like a serial, and keep him all the while in ignorance of where they aim. Who are they, then? and who is the dreamer?
>
> Well, as regards the dreamer, I can answer that, for he is no less a person than myself ... And for the Little People, what shall I say they are but just my Brownies, God bless them! Who do one-half my work for me while I am fast asleep, and in all human likelihood, do the rest for me as well, when I am wide awake and fondly suppose I do it for myself. That part which is done when I am sleeping is the Brownies' part beyond contention; but that which is done when I am up and about is by no means necessarily mine, since all goes to show the Brownies have had a hand in it even then... the whole of my published fiction should be the single-handed product of some Brownie, some Familiar, some unseen collaborator, whom I keep locked in a back garret, while I get the praise and he but a share (which I cannot prevent him getting) of the pudding. (A Chapter on Dreams)

RLS believed in his and other people's psychic powers. He knew there was a force beyond himself that affected his writings and the behaviour of others about him. He became for a short while secretary of the Edinburgh Psychic Society and although little is known of his activities, the interest showed itself through his writings for the rest of his life.

Long after I had closed the shop in Scotland, an opportunity presented itself to visit Western Samoa. A long time wish fulfilled, I climbed laboriously to the top of Mount Vaea, under the blazing noontide sun to Stevenson's grave. The heat and humidity were remorseless and without the benefit of insect repellant or sun screen I was bitten, sunburned, exhausted and truly sorry I had come! Yet, once at the summit I sat down on the cool concrete, in the Samoan fashion, alone and at peace. I gazed out over the harbour of Apia and out to sea and almost in a dream took out my notebook. I wrote effortlessly and without pausing for over twenty minutes, so quickly I hardly knew what was on the page (see 'The Last Word', for which I have no explanation for what was written, nor why I had to write, other than an urgency to do so).

The Samoans believe that Stevenson's house 'Vailima' is haunted both with their own 'aitus' (ghosts) and Tusitala. The locals have heard, on more than one occasion, strange noises in the great hall at a time of night when it was unoccupied. Sounds of a party; clinking of glasses, laughter and merry making. The Malietos daughter, in residence at Vailima in her childhood, reported seeing Tusitala at the foot of her bed.

'He seemed to be trying to tell me something, but I was too afraid to listen and I hid under the covers,' she said. 'I am sorry now. What was it that he so badly wanted to say?'

What comes through to us, I wondered, despite any block we might put in the way of an acknowledgement, that cannot be totally explained. Was there a Stevenson that wanted to be heard now: Had he written of things long ago that were meant for today's reader? Problems that he recognised then are still relevant today. Was it more than chance that I had walked into the shop on Victoria Street via Monterey?

On the trip to Samoa in 1991, I knew there was unfinished business with Stevenson. Only part of his message had been heard. There was much more to be learned; more of life and joy, forbearance and fun. Especially fun! Perhaps for all of us that is the real message from the man himself. To live life to the fullest, not hang back; accept ourselves for who we are and share above all else, share ourselves and our joy with the world.

Then to republish and exalt in the volumes of his works available to us. Going into the new century the words stand with the same relevancy today as they did a hundred years ago. In Stevenson's own words: *A knowledge that another has felt as we have felt, and seen things, even as they are little things, not much otherwise than we have seen them, will continue to the end to be one of life's choicest pleasures.*

NICHOLAS RANKIN

LIVES IN LONDON, WRITING & PRESENTING RADIO FOR BBC WORLD SERVICE · MARRIED TO NOVELIST MAGGIE GEE, WITH SEVEN-YEAR OLD DAUGHTER, ROSA

BORN: 1950, KENYA. EDUCATION: SHREWSBURY & OXFORD · WORKED IN SOUTH AMERICA & SPAIN · TRAVELLED TO SAMOA FOR BOOK DEAD MAN'S CHEST: TRAVELS AFTER ROBERT LOUIS STEVENSON

TRAVELS AFTER STEVENSON

TRAVELS AFTER STEVENSON

NICHOLAS RANKIN

Doubtless the world is quite right in a million ways; but you have to be kicked about a little to convince you of the fact. And in the meanwhile you must do something, be something, believe something. It is not possible to keep the mind in a state of accurate balance and blank; and even if you could do so, instead of coming ultimately to the right conclusion, you would be very apt to remain in a state of balance and blank to perpetuity.

VIRGINIBUS PUERISQUE:

CRABBED AGE & YOUTH

A summer thunderstorm flooded part of the garage and soaked the bottom of the stack. I operated on three wet boxes with a Stanley knife and rescued scores of damp Faber paperbacks by Caesarean section. They were my babies: the last remaining stock of my first and (so far) only book, 'Dead Man's Chest: Travels after Robert Louis Stevenson' (1987). Dabbing at Dan Fern's bright covers with a cloth took me back the ten years or so to how it all began. And it reminded me how much I owe to Robert Louis Stevenson. He changed my life.

The genesis of 'Dead Man's Chest' is related in the Prologue to the book. The great Argentine writer Jorge Luis Borges came to London to give a lecture and, knowing that he was blind, I took some books to his hotel to read to him. In a 1960 essay 'Borges and I' he had written 'I like hourglasses, maps, eighteenth-century typography, the roots of words, the taste of coffee, and Stevenson's prose.' I read Borges some of Stevenson's marvellous *Fables;* he gave me a small stone. When I told this to the publisher Robert McCrum he asked me to write a travel book following RLS from Edinburgh to Samoa.

It was late autumn 1983, and the commission came like a bolt of grace from heaven. I was thirty-three years old and, if not quite a failure in life, had demonstrably not found my way. I was scratching a living reviewing, teaching English, and interpreting Spanish for the Metropolitan Police. For fifteen years my secret ambition had been to write, but I had only published one short story and had a play performed by a fringe theatre group: very small beer in Grub Street. And then this. You only ever get two such opportunities in your whole life, my Scottish grandfather used to say, and I knew this was make or break for me. So I went for it with all my heart.

I had married the writer Maggie Gee in the summer of 1983, and in 1984 a new chapter opened for us. I became a Stevensonian that year, reading everything by and about RLS that I could lay my hands on. I went round the world following him — to Scottish islands and lighthouses, to English villages and London clubs, through French woods and faded seaside resorts, across neon America by bus to California where Stevenson had travelled for love. I saw his cigarette burns on a mantelpiece, found an 1896 newspaper in a pair of his old boots. I was chased by dogs, bitten by a Hawaiian horse, haunted by ghosts. I sat in his buttoned armchair in Sydney, slept in houses where he'd lived, walked on his verandahs and climbed up the mountain in Western Samoa to where he is buried. And I was steeped in his writing. I passed with colours an informal seven-hour viva voce examination by Ernest Mehew — 'the Mycroft Holmes of Stevensonians' — and the editor of RLS's letters. I thought I knew it all. But I still had not written a word of the book.

My wife rescued me. As a practising novelist Maggie Gee knew that 'research' — the bliss of loafing, reading, travelling, sleuthing, talking — is not the half of it; books mean bums on chairs at desks. She rented a flat at the foot of Boscombe Chine (the other end of Bournemouth from where the Stevensons lived from 1884 to 1887) and chained me to my desk. There and back in London the book took me a year and a half to write. I smoked a pack of Marlboros a day, and by the end I felt old and grey and utterly wrung-out. I swore I'd never write another book ever again, and so far I've kept my word, although I am back to the comfortable illusion that I could if I really wanted to.

'Dead Man's Chest' was published in hardback that summer of 1987, in paperback in autumn 1988. For a first book it was lucky, in reviews, in sales, in letters from unknown readers around the world. And the book also led to the second great opportunity of my life.

On Monday May 19 1986 (the Stevensons' 106th wedding anniversary) there was an ad in the Media section of 'The Guardian' for a Scriptwriter in the Central Talks and Features Department of the BBC External Services at Bush House. I'm sure that the forthcoming book gave me a tiny edge as a candidate. Five months later I began working for the World Service and I have been there ever since, and have travelled for them to China and Rumania, Spain and North America, making programmes about 'a number of things' including blind people, books, baobab trees and American Indian braves. Stevenson helped me to achieve a status and define a self.

RLS charms you into thinking that your relation with him is unique. He casts a spell of intimacy over readers. Those English people who call all emotion 'sentimentality' tend to suspect 'charm', but it is a rare literary quality that Stevenson himself esteemed. Henry James called RLS 'a Scotsman of the world' and it is wonderful to see how readers outside the UK respond to the quality of Stevenson. I'm thinking of the indefatigable Michel Le Bris in France, and in the Spanish-speaking world not just Borges in Argentina, but Guillermo Cabrera Infante from Cuba, the film-maker Raul Ruiz from Chile, the writer and philosopher Fernado Savater in Spain (whose outstanding essays on Stevenson are not, to my knowledge, yet available in English).

Stevenson possessed me for a time, though I don't feel that I possess him, or that I ever did. But he's become a lifelong interest for me. I collect Stevensonia, in a modest way, and try to keep up with the scholarship. What I am really looking forward to in the centenary year is the Collected Letters of RLS, edited by Ernest Mehew for Yale University Press. There will be your true Stevenson, the man himself, by his own hand. Those who always told me that he was second-rate will see that the most reliable of critics, posterity, has not found him wanting.

I have forgotten much of what I once knew about Robert Louis Stevenson but what I can remember will stay with me for life. Time wears things down to their essence. And what remains for me of Stevenson, apart from the immediate youthful charm, that bright ring of words? His wisdom about life, I think: that life is precious and brief and is to be lived; that you should live through your ages fully as they pass, that *Danger, enterprise, hope, the novel, the aleatory, are dearer to man than regular meals,* that life is battle, but there is joy in that battle, and going down doesn't matter if you've done what you think is right. I like it that he wasn't a prig about his principles, that he wasn't racist or sexist, that he liked plants but was hopeless at identifying trees, that he could sympathise with all kinds and conditions of creatures: snails, mice, dogs, people, a baboon called Jacko. I like his Great Heart.

I see him mostly in tropical whites with his cheese-cutter-brim yachting 'kepi'. He is the Lean Man of the later years, thin head, dark hair and moustache, wise eyes. He is booted to ride old Jack down the rocky road from Vailima to Apia where there's another political row. It's steamy hot in the tropics but there's shade on the verandah and you can see the sun shine on the water out to the reef. I talk to him with respect always. Even if I outlive his forty-four years, he will always be my elder and better. I call him in the Spanish way 'mi general' and he is still my hero.

NEIL WILKIE

BROADCASTER OF SHORT STORIES, FEATURES AND STAGE MUSICALS · LATEST COMPLETED WORK A MUSICAL PLAY ON ROBERT LOUIS STEVENSON: TELLER OF TALES

UNITED NATIONS AGENCIES CONSULTANT FOR OVER 20 YEARS IN INTERNATIONAL DEVELOPMENT FOR FAO, THE WORLD BANK & UNICEF · WORKED IN AFRICA, MIDDLE EAST AND LATIN AMERICA ON CHILD HEALTH & NUTRITION

ACCENTS OF THE MIND

ACCENTS OF THE MIND
NEIL WILKIE

I think we all belong to many countries, and perhaps this habit of much travel, and the engendering of scattered friendships, may prepare the euthanasia of ancient nations.

SILVERADO SQUATTERS

We soared through the bubbles of cumulus shrouding Madagascar and veered northward into the night. It was the end of a long mission; mind and body were due for a rest. But this time the midnight theatre of my brain (I was to take up the phrase later, from Stevenson) was reluctant to close. Leaving the beautiful land of the lemurs, I was still sifting strategies for agricultural reform, debating with Government officials, standing in a warehouse on a mountain of unsold cloves. I tried leaning back, lolling at my window, and watched the starboard wing-light flashing its amber signal in the void. This was a familiar trick, the pulsating blink always gently hypnotic. But other images leapt to mind from twenty years of travel for the United Nations. The ragged shanty-dwellers of Pernambuco... emaciated village elders clamouring for their forest road in Cameroon... the cries of malnourished babies in Berber tents... Criss-crossing frontiers, switching languages... The amber signal kept flashing messages. A hundred journeys. Sixty countries. Too many messages. Under the weather, or over the hill? Perhaps, I thought, it's time to stop. Be a tourist on a beach. Or change direction. Start a development project of my own...

The plane rumbled over the Thames and taxied into Heathrow. Another lightning stopover in a country I once knew well. Another snatched visit to a West End bookshop.

Idly glancing at an upper shelf, I reached for the paperback with the reassuring title: *The Amateur Emigrant*. Curious. So this was by Robert Louis Stevenson? But why the Statue of Liberty on the cover — what was *his* American connection? Intriguing. I paid at the desk and caught the next nine-hour bus ride back to Washington, the quintessential transit lounge that served as home.

One sultry evening by the Potomac — it was some weeks later (August 29, 1985, my diary tells me) — I turned to *The Amateur Emigrant,* boarded the Devonia and sailed off down the Clyde with him to California. Stevenson wrote many more famous books, but for me this account of his six-thousand-mile journey in pursuit of Fanny Osbourne has the epic quality of a pageant. Back in 1879 the first draft struck Colvin, Stevenson's mentor, as 'a somewhat wordy and spiritless record of squalid experiences', and his furious father paid promptly to stop its publication. Jonathan Raban has called it 'a living nightmare, and a masterpiece'. My first sensation on reading it was sheer elation. From where I sat, at a midpoint in Stevenson's odyssey, it was easy to feel at the heart of it. But with this narrator, in limbo with an international assortment of fellow travellers, I began to feel something more. It was in the nature of a homecoming.

Being half a Scot and half a Manxman, I held no chauvinistic reverence for my birthplace in England. To reach school in Liverpool I had walked daily through the Indian quarter, the Chinese quarter and the black quarter. My father's letters, written with the sure hand of a marine engineer, came bearing postmarks from Karachi and Capetown, Singapore and San Francisco. With these beginnings, the globe seemed to me an interesting neighbourhood to live and work in. When the opportunity knocked I was happy enough to earn a United Nations address. I felt that I fitted in, which is what was so remarkable to me about the Stevenson of 1879. Here was an adventurous and genial spirit, devoid of snobbery, contemptuous of racial and religious bigotry, who understood the anonymity of exile but learned to thrive on it. With RLS my 'sense of kinship' (to use his phrase, writing of the Marquesan islanders) was profound. And energizing. I was moved and thrilled by the theatrical qualities of the book, and fascinated by the tale of true romance underlying the travelogue. I felt a kind of wild excitement I hadn't experienced since the sixties. Foolishly, at that moment I called to my wife: 'What a story! Now this would make a musical'. I think she knew then that I was going to write it.

Until that evening my knowledge of Stevenson and his works bordered on zero. In my urban childhood no doting aunt had shown me the garden of verses. As a student of literature in the fifties I had alighted on *Virginibus Puerisque* at Cambridge, but without loitering; it was a time when RLS was ignored by the academics *in situ*, and David Daiches, staunch Stevensonian, had barely arrived at the lecturer's podium to suggest otherwise. Films were to frame my memories of *Treasure Island* and the unfortunate Dr Jekyll, enlivened by Robert Newton's rolling eyes and Spencer Tracy flailing through the fogs of Soho. I knew nothing yet of the Stevenson family of engineers, although my own seafaring forbears from the Mearns will have been guided home by Stevenson lighthouses. And of RLS's audacious life, both before and after the dramatic entrance of Fanny Osbourne, I had everything to learn. The idea of preparing RLS for the musical stage was more than an absorbing challenge. Like Don Quixote's impossible dream it was soon to become a quest, and would be pursued with something akin to passion.

A musical celebration of RLS — a man so rich in character, a life so highly spiced — called for a gourmet recipe. Research was the key ingredient and I was already ravenous. For the next three crowded years daily duties were sandwiched with a new pleasure. RLS became my constant travelling companion, his writings my daily read. On journeys to Bolivia and West Africa, Stevenson essays and letters were eagerly crammed between files of economic data and social surveys. His correspondence with Charles Baxter was plundered on a plateau in the Andes, his *Memories and Portraits* beside the Gulf of Guinea. My next exit from the land of the lemurs was the cue to rummage in one more biography. Spare time was sought

and found where there was none before. My family were
bemused, but my wife was already packing. Off-duty on the
Pacific coast, we followed the RLS trail that curved through
California from Silverado to the mountains above Carmel. We
traced the ruined cabin, unmarked by San Clemente creek,
where RLS, delirious and dying, was saved for posterity and
ultimate success *by an old frontiersman, a mighty hunter of bears.* In
Monterey, the Old Pacific Capital which so treasures the stay of
Stevenson, we lingered beyond a week. When family circumstances eventually prescribed farewell to Washington, our
return to old Europe and to the decayed fabric of 'Mrs
Thatcher's Britain', the trauma was mitigated among the
wynds of Edinburgh and by the bridge at Grèz-sur-Loing.

The irony of it all was transparent. As a self styled 'amateur
emigrant', Stevenson had left Scotland, abandoned friends
and risked his career in journeying west across the Atlantic.
His years of deep involvement in affairs of social and economic development were still to come, among the lepers of
Molokai and the plantations of Samoa. I had moved in the
reverse direction. By January 1989 I had kicked over the last
traces of an international career, bid goodbye to the colleagues and friends of twenty years, quit America and, in a
country awash with new values, begun digging around ances-
tral roots in Caledonia. The landscape seemed bare of familiar faces. The unknown beckoned. In such circumstances I
took the tip from RLS and plunged headlong into writing.
Within a month I had sketched out my musical play, inspired
by his colourful life. Book, lyrics and a draft music score
began emerging into daylight. Two years on, the transition
was complete. I had made a host of new friends, and the
work on *Teller of Tales* was done.

But was my journey really necessary? I have since met scep-
tics, starry-eyed at the mere mention of Stevenson, whose
twinkling orbs turn bleary at the sound of 'a musical'. About
RLS? *Why* a musical? I share the fear of sacrilege. A vision of
robotic roller-skaters encircling Mt. Vaea or kilted chorus-lines
capering over the Pentlands can indeed cause palpitations.
The rationale goes deeper. We know that musical perfor-

mance was never RLS' forte — how could it be, given his gamut of other dazzling talents? — but few memorable figures have displayed a youthful zest and wit and warmth so fitting to the spirit of music. RLS himself thought so. At twenty-two, jubilant after a night at the theatre he declared that 'an opera is far more *real* than real life to me', and wrote breathlessly from Frankfurt to his mother:

> I wish that life was an opera. I should like to live in one; but I don't know in what quarter of the globe I shall find a society so constituted... imagine asking for three-kreuzer cigars in recitative, or giving the washerwoman the inventory of your dirty clothes in a sustained and flourishous aria.

Fighting every illness with buoyant optimism, he would go on to fill his life with as much drama, romance and *real* heroism as perhaps any opera could contain. 'That he was musical at all will probably be regarded as a revelation to most people', wrote a 'Glasgow Herald' contributor in 1900. But Stevenson's stepson-comrade Lloyd Osbourne would later recall 'how constantly he spoke of music', and that 'he bought an extraordinary amount of printed music... and would pore over it for hours at a time, trying here and there, with endless repetitions, to elucidate it with his flageolet'. RLS may have lacked musical credentials, but posterity need not doubt his inclinations. And as a student actor, mimic, raconteur and frequent stand-up comedian of the day, a 'born entertainer' in the eyes of his contemporaries, he has impressive qualifications to appear at centre-stage. 'The talent was in the personality', wrote Jenni Calder in her life study of RLS; 'the genius lay in who and what he was, rather than in the products of his pen'. Therein may lie the strongest clue to his abiding popularity.

I suppose I have now read, and enjoyed, almost everything that Stevenson wrote. But it is 'who and what he was' that won my esteem and will continue to hold my affection. I have never been a hunter after heroes (or 'role models', as our inventive age prefers to call them), yet I like to think that RLS was, and is, a hero for our time. Vision, courage, compassion and that prized 'sense of kinship' he had in abundance. He fought for his own independence of mind and spirit, accepting no one else's creed, devising his own code of morality. For children and all 'underdogs' he had instinctive sympathy. He argued women's causes long before they erupted as feminism, and his concern for justice would mobilize every skill at his command to condemn detractors of the leper missionary Father Damien, the cynicism of the colonial powers in Samoa, and *the millionaire vulgarians of the Big Bonanza*.

A man with that reach of imagination could love humanity in any corner of the globe. Artificial national or ethnic barriers would be no obstacle to friendship. He could always see the other side.

IAN NIMMO

BORN: INDIA · EDUCATED: DUNKELD, BREADALBANE · COMMISSIONED IN ROYAL SCOTS FUSILIERS · FORMER EDITOR WEEKLY SCOTSMAN · EDITOR EVENING NEWS

PUBLICATIONS: ROBERT BURNS—HIS LIFE AND TRADITIONS ; CROSSING THE TAY; PORTRAIT OF EDINBURGH, THE BRAVE ADVENTURE; SCOTLAND AT WAR & EDINBURGH — THE NEW TOWN

THE RLS OMISSION

THE RLS OMISSION
IAN NIMMO

Of all places for a view, this Calton Hill is perhaps the best; since you can see the Castle, which you lose from the Castle, and Arthur's Seat, which you cannot see from Arthur's Seat. It is the place to stroll on one of those days of sunshine and east wind which are so common in our more than temperate summer.

The scene suggests reflections on fame and on man's injustice to the dead.

EDINBURGH: PICTURESQUE NOTES

One of the talking points about Scotland's capital is its plethora of monuments and statues to famous sons. As you would expect from our ancient city, where the story of Scotland itself virtually unfolded around its castle, palace and closes, where many of our historical figures stepped its streets, Edinburgh fairly bristles with memorials to them. Although erecting statues to the famous has become unfashionable they nonetheless lend atmosphere, eloquence and grace to the city.

But apart from the houses where Robert Louis Stevenson once lived, there is little in Edinburgh to commemorate him. Yet surely he remains one of Edinburgh's and Scotland's most famous and best loved writers, with a foot on the world stage.

It may be that Scotland's capital, even unconsciously, has never quite forgiven him for his love-hate relationship with his city or pointing an accusatory finger at the pomposity and hypocrisy that was part and parcel of 19th century Edinburgh, some of which lingers to this day. Whatever the reason, R.L.S. has never been properly recognised by his city — as Sir Walter

Scott was recognised, and whose Monument dominates the main thoroughfare in Princes Street.

Personally, I don't like to see Stevenson diminished in this manner. Of couse, I am full of admiration for the concept and sentiment behind Ian Cameron Finlay's Princes Street Gardens birches, a special kind of memorial, with its linked bequest to children suffering from respiratory diseases, an achievement which took an enormous effort and dedication by many people. But in recent times lifesize statues have been erected to such as 'Bomber' Harris, leveller of German cities in World War Two, to a footballer in Newcastle and to Arthur Conan Doyle in Edinburgh, whose links with the city are surface rooted to say the least. I therefore asked the question in my book on Edinburgh's New Town whether the Princes Street Garden's memorial is now enough? In fact, has Edinburgh ever done enough for Robert Louis Stevenson?

I accept entirely his own opinion on statues, as set out so emphatically in his letter to Charles Baxter regarding the request for a donation for a memorial to James Ballantyne, the publisher. Basically, in that particular case, RLS did not approve. Nor did he like self-publicity.

But RLS was also not without his pride and vanity or his desire for recognition as a writer. There was an indication of his thinking in his idea of repairing Robert Fergusson's headstone in the Canongate Kirkyard, originally erected and paid for by Robert Burns. RLS who was fascinated by the thought of Scotland's *three Robbies* — Fergusson, Burns and Stevenson — considered rededicating the headstone with an inscription to include his own name along the lines of *a gift from one Edinburgh lad to another*.

RLS was not entirely averse to a stone recognition with the right inscription. And, who knows, as the years passed, he may well have changed his mind about statues? Or his sentiments could have been disregarded and the matter taken out of his hands as happens so often with public figures. The key point is that for a writer of Stevenson's stature in his own city, that claims to nurture the arts, RLS goes unrecognised in the monument stakes.

Then I got to thinking. And I remembered when I was editor for six years of the evening newspaper in Teesside, that rumbustious, highly industralised, bucking bronco of an area in North Yorkshire. Just behind Teesside, on the edge of the Yorkshire Moors, there is a range of hills very much like our own Pentlands, called the Cleveland Hills. On top of one of them is a tall, stately, rough-stone cairn about 50 feet in height, visible for 10 miles round.

'Oh, didn't you know?' I was told. 'That's Captain Cook's Monument. He was a local lad and it was built as a mark of respect by the readers of your newspaper.' Many years before readers responded magnificently to an appeal by the paper to commemorate the great voyager by humping rocks to the summit to build a simple cairn to him. Families, schools, clubs, groups and individuals trekked up with their stones or hired transport to carry the bigger ones. A local builder bound the rocks together out of goodwill and the whole exercise took little time and cost precisely nothing. But it did give an enormous sense of achievement and satisfaction to the whole community who point it out today with genuine pride.

I see no reason why a similar exercise could not be successfully mounted in Edinburgh to mark Robert Louis Stevenson's centenary.

Carrying a stone to build a cairn is a time-honoured mark of respect around the world. But this cairn would be no ordinary monument. I quote from my book: 'It should be a hundred feet high at least, placed on an appropriate vantage point so that it can be seen for miles around, a new talking point on the Edinburgh scene, for the city as well as the tourists, a place to visit as a prominent and significant Edinburgh feature to Robert Louis Stevenson, somewhere high so that it can be looked up to.' And when visitors ask local people what the cairn represents, the answer should be pat: 'That's what Edinburgh and Scotland did for RLS'

Personally, I would place it on Arthur's Seat, high over his city and looking out to sea and to the hills that meant so much to him. Almost 200 years ago John Ruskin thought that would be the best site for Walter Scott's 'small, vulgar, Gothic steeple'.

Of course there are other sites. The Calton Hill for one, that *'field of munuments'* as Stevenson called his favourite prospect of Edinburgh. There remains plenty of room on its summit. Or on top of Caerketton or Allermuir in the Pentlands, both favoured haunts where he once expressed the wish to be buried like a Covenanter. Or Swanston where he was happy in childhood. Or out at Glencorse, a special place he indicated to Samuel Crocket: *'Do you know where the road crosses the burn under Glencorse church? Go there and say a prayer for me: moriturus salutat. See that it's a sunny day; I would like it to be a Sunday... stand on the right hand bank just where the road goes down into the water, and shut your eyes and see if I don't appear to you!'*

There would be no shortage of vounteers to build a Stevenson cairn. His old school, the Edinburgh Academy would play a part, others schools might want to be involved; students from Edinburgh University, his university, could carry a stone and perhaps even raise money for charity at the same time. And if one of the charities to benefit was for children with respiratory illnesses so much the better. Colleges, companies, clubs, businesses, families might all want to help and if the local newspapers threw their weight behind such a scheme, organising or sponsoring an appeal to readers to bring a stone to build a cairn* for Robert Louis Stevenson, this would be appropriate and something special and imaginative to mark the centenary. There is so much goodwill towards him to be tapped.

'Robert Louis Stevenson (1850-1894). Erected in memory of RLS by the citizens of Edinburgh' would not only be a fitting inscription on a tablet but would also fulfil Stevenson's wish that it be 'simple and heartfelt'.

* *(a site on Calton Hill is now under discussion)*

149

LLOYD OSBOURNE

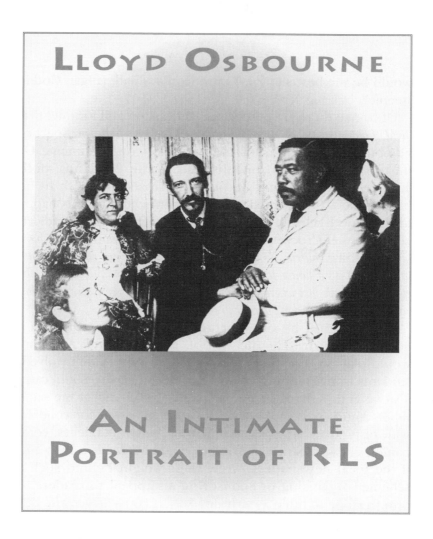

AN INTIMATE
PORTRAIT OF RLS

STEVENSON AT THIRTY-EIGHT

I n 1888, Saranac was a little backwoods settlement in which
log cabins were common, and venison one of the staples of
diet. On the edge of the Canadian border, and encompassed by
a trackless country of woods and lakes called 'the Adirondack
Wilderness,' it had in winter the isolation of an outpost of the
snows. Red-hot stoves and streaming windows; guides who
spat, and looked like Leatherstocking; consumptives in bright
caps and many-hued woollens gaily tobogganing at forty below
zero; buffalo coats an inch thick; snow-storms, snow-drifts,
Arctic cold; of such was our new home in which RLS was hop-

ing to regain his health.

We had rented the half of a small house which stood bald and isolated on a bluff overlooking the river and was the kind of house that a prosperous guide would run up in his spare time with the help of a local carpenter. Its lack of conveniences may be imagined; except for the organ in the 'parlor' it was starkly primitive. At times it was unbelievably cold, when one was really comfortable only in bed, with a hot soapstone at one's feet. We had made the mistake — or at least our neigbors had shaken their heads over it — of not blocking the big fireplace in our sitting-room, where we had our meals and spent most of our time.

During the blizzards we were chilled to the marrow of our bones. The only fresh air that ever entered the place was down our despised chimney, and often the hearth before the fire was the coldest spot in the house.

Colorado had been foregone for Saranac, then in the beginning of its vogue as a cure for tuberculosis. RLS arrived there in an exhilaration of mind which of itself was likely to help him as much as the climate. When he stepped off our old cattle-boat, the *Ludgate Hill*, in which we had taken nineteen days to cross the Atlantic, it was to find himself famous. Hordes of reporters met him; the lobby of this hotel buzzed with callers; he was head-lined in all the papers — interviewed, photographed, lionized — his coming a veritable sensation. His reputation, silently spreading, silently infiltrating through a vast public, had suddenly with a universal acclaim risen to a place second to no novelist's in England or America.

He was almost dumbfounded; it was too incredible for belief; and at first he was inclined to ascribe it to American exuberance. But it was no flash in the pan, no temporary manifestation of excited journalism. It began to reverberate back from England and took on the very convincing form of big cheques and dazzling offers. From that time until his death he became, indeed, one of the most conspicuous figures in contemporary literature. That he enjoyed this sudden elevation goes without saying. He exulted in it; it did much to keep him alive; it gave him an assurance and an authority he had never felt before. In those nineteen days on the *Ludgate Hill*, he had passed from one epoch of his life to another. The recluse of 'Skerryvore,' working so hard in fancied obscurity, had sprung at a bound into world-wide fame.

Saranac suited RLS extremely well. He gained weight; his spectral aspect disappeared; in a buffalo coat and astrakhan cap he would pace the veranda for hours, inhaling that piercing air which was so noticeably benefiting him. He worked hard, hard and well, first on a series of essays for *Scribner's Magazine* then, at the close of our stay and in a whirlwind three weeks of industry, on the *Wrong Box* — my own book, which had cost me a winter's toil.

This collaboration, if so it may be called, was conceived on the spur of the moment. RLS had finished the reading of my final draft, and I was sitting on the side of his bed in no little suspense for his verdict. It meant a great deal to me, for S.S. McClure had promised to publish the book if RLS thought it good enough.

'Lloyd, it is really not at all bad,' he said musingly. 'Some of it is devilishly funny; and I have burst out laughing again and again; your dialogue is often better than I could have done myself at thirty; there is no reason at all why McClure should not bring it out, and with any luck it might be a very successful book.'

Then after a pause, he added, through the faint cloud of his cigarette smoke: 'But of course it is unequal; some of it is pretty poor; and what is almost worse is the good stuff you have wasted — thrown away — just because you didn't know how to use it. It made my fingers itch as I read it. Why, I could take up that book, and in one quick, easy rewriting could make it *sing!*'

Our eyes met; it was all decided in that one glance.

'By God, why shouldn't I!' he exclaimed. 'That is if you don't mind?'

Mind!

I was transported with joy. What would-be writer of nineteen would not have been? It was my vindication; the proof I had not been living in a fool's paradise, and had indeed talent, and a future.

McClure, to whom I have just alluded, was then in the beginning of his meteoric career. He was ready at a moment's notice to take fire with excitement and to soar into the azure of dreams and millions from which Stevenson had constantly to pull him down by the legs, so to speak.

But to one of his many plans RLS responded with unqualified enthusiasm — to charter a large yacht, and to sail away for half a year or more in the Indian or Pacific Oceans, supporting the enterprise by monthly letters, which McClure was to syndicate at enormous mutual profit, guaranteed beforehand. It was undeniably practicable — no azure here, no pulling down of those slender legs — all RLS had to say was which ocean and when.

RLS had set his heart on the Pacific, but as there seemed no likelihood whatever of finding a suitable yacht in San Francisco, it looked as though he would have to content himself with the Indian Ocean. There was a wealth of vessels to be had on the Eastern seaboard; and McClure, in paroxysms of excitement, was indefatigably submitting lists, with aides out in every direction combing all the ports from Maine to Florida. A ship was a ship to McClure, and in the same letter and with the same conviction he would proffer a floating steam palace of three thousand tons and a duckshooting forty-footer, 'with a nest of dories.' I remember the unextinguishable laughter we had over this last sentence. 'They sound like some kind of birds,' wrote McClure, 'but perhaps you will know what is meant..'

When my mother left us in the Spring to visit her sister in California, our plans were so definitely leading toward the Indian Ocean that it was only in a joking spirit that RLS had said at parting:

'If you should *find a yacht out there, mind you take it.'*

Six weeks later came the telegram that was to have such a far-reaching effect on our lives:

'Can secure splendid sea-going schooner yacht Casco for seven hundred and fifty a month with most comfortable accommodation for six aft and six forward. Can be ready for sea in ten days. Reply immediately. FANNY.'

Stevenson answered:

'Blessed girl, take the yacht and expect us in ten days. LOUIS.'

STEVENSON AT THIRTY-NINE

Waikiki in 1889 consisted of twenty or thirty houses, set in large shady gardens, and bordering on the most incomparably lovely beach in the world — and the most incomparable water to swim in, four miles from Honolulu. RLS rented a house, and moved ashore from the *Casco* with everything we possessed.

The characteristic feature of an Hawaiian house is the *lanai*, or big sitting-room, without walls on one or two sides — trellises of creepers and flowers taking their place. This summer-house arrangement is only possible in such a perfect climate, and is extraordinarily pleasant to live in.

Our Chinese cook, Ah Fu, had followed us from the yacht — a powerfully-built, frowsy-haired sort of Man Friday, not over twenty-five, who had been marooned as a boy on Hiva Oa, and was much more of a Marquesan than he was anything else.

The seven months' cruise just concluded had had a marvellous effect on RLS. He had become almost well; could ride, take long walks, dine out, and in general lead the life of a man in ordinary health. Such climates were supposed to be very harmful for tubercular patients, whom the local doctors sent away at once — but Stevenson throve. His fine complexion had regained its ruddy tint; his hair, now cut short, was no longer lank, but glossy and of a lighter brown; his eyes, always his most salient feature and always brilliant, had no longer that strange fire of disease; he walked with a firm, light step, and, though to others he must have appeared thin and fragile, to us the transformation in him was astounding. In his soft white shirt, blue serge coat, white flannel trousers, white shoes, and white yachting cap (such caps were his favorites till his death) he looked to perfection the famous author who had arrived in a yacht, and who 'dressed the rôle,' as actors say, in a manner worthy of his dashing schooner.

It was typical of Stevenson that instead of choosing the best room in the house for his own he should seek out a dilapidated, cobwebby little shack, thirty or forty yards away, and papered with mildewed newspapers, in which to install himself. Here in complete contentment with his cot, flageolet, and ink-bottle, he set himself to the task of finishing the *Master of Ballantrae* — while centipedes wriggled unnoticed on his floor, lizards darted after flies, and the undisturbed spiders peacefully continued the weaving of their webs. Here King Kalakaua would occasionally drop in on him for a long and confidential talk, while the horses of the royal equipage flicked their tails under a neighboring tree, and the imposing coachman and footman dozed on their box.

King Kalakaua, the last of the Hawaiian kings, was a much-maligned man, highly-educated with an air of extreme distinction and a most winning graciousness and charm. He would have been at ease in any court in Europe. Stevenson and he became great friends, finding their strongest bond in Polynesian lore and antiquities. This grave, earnest, rather careworn man (dressed usually in the most faultless of white flannels,) seldom came to see us without his chamberlain carrying books, and always urging Stevenson to 'stay and make your home with us. Hawaii needs you.'

This home, wherever it was going to be, was causing Stevenson a good deal of concern. At first he anticipated returning to England; in fact for a while this was as good as settled; 'Skerryvore' was still there, temporarily rented, and absence, perhaps, was endowing it with a certain glamour. But most compelling of all, I think, was RLS's desire to stroll into the Savile Club and electrify all his old friends as the returned seafarer from the South Sea Islands. At least he was constantly dwelling on this phase of his return, and choosing the exact hour when he could make the most dramatic entrance. But as the conviction grew that he never could be so well as in the Pacific, and with the vague and romantic idea of finding an island of his own, he began to talk of another cruise and to look about for the means.

The means, alas, were strictly limited to one ship, the missionary vessel, *Morning Star*, which in a few months' time was due to start on her annual tour of mission stations. Her itinerary was extraordinarily attractive; she went to many of the wildest and least-known islands of the Western Pacific; but her drawbacks were frightful — no smoking, not a drink, no profanity; church, nightly prayer-meetings and an enforced intimacy with the most uncongenial people.

American missionaries often are excessively narrow, intolerant, and puritanical; the prospect of four months in their society calculated to make the stoutest heart quail. But for us it was the *Morning Star* or nothing; and RLS, who was not without adroitness, began to cultivate the necessary acquaintances and pull the necessary wires — with the result that at last we were accepted, though reluctantly, as passengers on the conditions I have indicated.

Our stay in Waikiki was not only note-worthy for RLS's decision to remain permanently in the Pacific but, for me at least, by a delightful change in our relations. We had started to collaborate on a book together, and after outlining and chapterizing it with much care I set to work on the first three chapters ultimately published under the name of the *Ebb Tide.* It went along swimmingly, and earning RLS's undiminished commendation until I reached the end of the present book, which was originally conceived as a prologue to a much longer novel. Then the commendation ceased; try as I would I could not please RLS; I wrote and rewrote, and rewrote again, but always to have him shake his head. Finally at his suggestion and in utter hopelessness I laid the manuscript by, hoping to come back to it later with greater success. But I never did. The novel was long and involved; it attracted us less and less and finally was tacitly abandoned, and we forgot all about it.

Several years afterward, Sir Graham Balfour, then on a visit to us at Vailima, unearthed the original manuscript, read it with enthusiasm, and amazed us by declaring it to be a story in itself, which with a few changes at the end, could be published as it stood. RLS, greatly doubting, read it again, and immediately taking fire rewrote the whole copy. Thus as a book it followed *The Wrecker,* though actually conceived and written before it.

To me, of our three collaborations, it was the most important of all, for it altered in a most unexpected way my whole relations with Stevenson. After it he regarded me seriously as a fellow-craftsman; sought my judgement and often took it.

One noonday RLS came driving in from Honolulu, his horses in a lather, and it needed but a single look at his face to see that he was wildly excited.

'*Have chartered a schooner!*' he shouted out before he even jumped down; and as we all crowded about him, he breathlessly continued; 'Arranged the details and signed the charter-party as she was casting off — tug tooting, and people pulling at the owner's coat-tails, and the sweat running of our faces in a tin office! The *Equator,* sixty-eight tons, and due back from San Francisco in a month to pick us up for the Gilbert Islands. Finest little craft you ever saw in your life, and I have the right to take her anywhere at so much a day!'

A hectic lunch followed: champagne was opened in honor of the occasion, and we drank to the *Equator* in foaming bumpers; everybody talked at once amid an unimaginable hilarity, for were we not to sail away in a vessel of our own, and freed from the nightmare of the *Morning Star?*

'And we can smoke on that blessed ship!' cried Stevenson, with uplifted glass.

'And drink' cried I. 'Hurrah for the *Equator!*'

'And swear!' exclaimed my mother delightfully — she who had never said 'damn' in her life.

Then at a yell from Ah Fu, and in a general outcry as he threw open the blinds on the seaward side, we looked out on one of the most inspiriting sights I have ever seen in my life — the *Equator* herself, under a towering spread of canvas, and as close in as her captain dared to put her, parting the blue water in flashes of spray on the way to San Francisco.

We were still watching when she broke out her ensign, and dipped it to us in farewell.

Our ship!

STEVENSON AT FORTY

An Apemama house of the kind corresponding to a 'smart, attractive, bijou little residence' with us, is a sort of giant clothes-basket of much the same color and wattle, with a peaked roof, and standing on stilts about a yard high. With a dozen pairs of human legs under it, you can steer it to any spot you like — provided it is level — and begin your modest housekeeping without further fuss.

We started ours in Apemama with four such houses, forty-eight pairs of legs, and the King, Winchester in hand, firing in the direction — but over the head — of any one who seemed backward. It was extremely disturbing at first to see that loaded rifle pointed hither and thither, and occasionally going off with a terrific report; but as nobody was ever hurt, and the work was certainly continued with feverish briskness, we were soon won over to think it quite a little help.

The King, handing his rifle with a negligent air to a trembling attendant, and ordering all the natives to withdraw to a little distance, walked in a big circle around the settlement, and declared it tabooed during our stay.

To pass the invisible line meant death, but whether from the rifle, or the outraged gods, was never very clear; but the important thing was that nobody ever did cross it except the King, who was privileged. Tembinoka was an out-and-out heathen, who had kept a missionary until he could learn English, and then had dismissed him with an emphatic warning never to come back. He was judge, jury, lawgiver, commander-in-chief, and unquestioned despot of three populous islands, and was a past master in kingcraft, both in its guile and in its public spirit. Christianity, as subversive of his authority, he had put aside as 'good for Kings, but bad for common people'; and in the same spirit of self-improvement with which he had welcomed the missionary, he consented to receive Stevenson, after it had been explained that the latter's stay was of a temporary nature only.

We were very happy in our little camp, which was delightful in every respect except for the flies. I built a little erection of camera-boxes by way of a desk for myself, and squatted uncomfortably in a corner. Here a large part of *The Wrecker* was written, and in that collaboration in spite of my cramped legs, I spent many of the pleasantest hours of my life.

It was exhilarating to work with Stevenson; he was so appreciative, so humorous — brought such gaiety, *camaraderie,* and good-will to our joint task. We never had a single disagreement as the book ran its course; it was a pastime, not a task, and I am sure no reader ever enjoyed it as much as we did. Well do I remember him saying: 'It's glorious to have the ground ploughed, and to sit back in luxury for the real fun of writing — which is rewriting.' In the evening when myriads of flies had given way to myriads of mosquitoes, and while we sat smoking round the lamp, safe within our net, he would review my work, read such of it as he had rewritten, and brightly discuss the chapter to come. Am I wrong in thinking that some of that zest is to be found in *The Wrecker*? It was conceived in such high spirits, and with so much laughter and entertainment. Every page of it was a joy — to us.

Our diet left much to be desired. Food was principally the long slimy slugs that were to be found on the beach, or anything in the way of a dead shark or a battered jelly-fish. Ah Fu fried them, grilled them, curried them, minced them; made them into game-pies, and heaven only knows what all — but the same seagull flavor was always there. Our flour was weevily, and in spite of careful sifting there were always dozens of little black threads in our bread, which when new was our greatest luxury — and which we buttered from a bottle. Butter of course, in that heat was a liquid. Our rice was as decayed as the flour, and similarly speckled. But we had plenty of good Californian claret, and on rare occasions sumptuous meals of turtle-steaks and soup.

We seldom walked anywhere except to the seaward side of the island, about half a mile distant. It was extraordinarily wild and solitary; nobody ever seemed to come here except our slave-girls, who trailed after us far behind, frolicking like puppies. Possibly they had been ordered to follow any of us leaving the camp. But ordered or not, they always did; and their favourite diversion was to strip off their last shred of clothing, and crowd all three of them, into some wretched little mud-puddle of fresh water on the way and with shouts of laughter, take what they considered to be a bath.

I have included Apemama in my papers as it was here Stevenson made two very important decisions. The first, to abandon the plan of buying a schooner of his own — which *The Wrecker* had been originally projected to pay for; and the second, the realization that if he were to make his home permanently in the Pacific it would have to be within reach of mails and amid a certain civilization. Our weeks of trading in the *Equator* had shown him the seamy side of such a life — the tricks, the false scales, the bamboozling and chicanery that were customary in dealing with the natives, who themselves were irritatingly dishonest.

His choice had narrowed to Suva, Honolulu, Papiete, or Apia, all of them in regular communication with the outside world; and as Samoa was the only conspicuous independent group left in the Pacific, and was renowned besides for its attractive and uncontaminated people — it was naturally this group that began to loom before us as our future home. Soon, indeed, we were studying the Samoan grammar and building fresh castles in the air.

Meanwhile we were growing increasingly anxious about the *Equator*. The three weeks had become six, and there was still no sign of her.

RLS, with some misgiving, explained the matter to the King. Had he any stores to spare, and might we draw on them? The King beamed at the request; it seemed to flatter him beyond measure to be asked such a favor. With a truly regal gesture he put his storehouses at our disposal. Their interiors presented an extraordinary sight as Ah Fu and I went into them to choose what we needed. Not only was there beef and pork, flour and rice, sugar, tea, coffee and other staples in prodigal profusion — but crates of mirrors, a large rocking-horse, French clocks with gilt cupids, baby-carriages, cut-glass bowls and vases, hand cultivators, plated-silver candelabra, silk parasols, framed chromos, toy steam-engines, ornate lamps, surgical-instruments cases, tea-baskets, sewing-machines — everything in fact that had ever caught Tembinoka's fleeting fancy in the trade-room of a ship, and all tumbled in pell-mell and some of it scarcely unpacked though once bought and placed here it had passed forever from his mind. As far as these objects had anything in common it was a general glitter and brightness. Apparently he had pointed his finger at anything that shone, and had said: 'I take that.'

A few days afterward a message from him brought us all in panting haste to his settlement. A vessel was coming in, and of course we were certain it was the *Equator*, and were correspondingly elated. But as she rose over the horizon of the vast lagoon, our glasses revealed her to be a stranger. What a disappointment! It seemed almost unbearable, but it was thrilling, nevertheless, to see that big unknown schooner sail in, and to hear the hoarse rush of her anchor-chain as we awaited her in a boat.

The *Tiernan* brought with her a new perplexity for us — should we try to charter her for Samoa, or should we gamble on the *Equator's* return? Were the latter indeed lost we might be marooned for half a year or more on our strip of coral. RLS, over our glasses of warm beer, went straight to the point; how much did he want — that brisk, little, whiskered captain in pyjamas — to carry us to Samoa?

Fortunately for us, his price was too high, although RLS remained a long time in indecision before finally refusing it. But if we did not sail in the *Tiernan* we at least drew liberally on her well-stocked trade-room. She then sailed away, to capsize subsequently in a squall, and drown a big portion of her complement, with a harrowing experience for her survivors, who nearly died of hunger and thirst before they reached land in her whale-boat. We often congratulated ourselves afterward that Captain Sach's terms had been so high; had they been more moderate we might all have perished.

Not long afterward we were gladdened by the sight of the *Equator*, which had been delayed by light airs and calms on her way back from Arorai Island. With what joy we shook our shipmates' hands and crowded round the table in her stuffy little cabin! It was home to us, and we looked about those familiar surroundings, small and mean though they have been, with an ecstatic contentment.

The next day we were packed up and aboard, and ready to sail with the out-going tide.

The King at parting grasped Stevenson's hand in both his arms, and said: 'Stevenson, you are a ver' good man. I think you are the best man I ever know,' and, with a pathos that was not a little moving, spoke of how he would always think of him and remember his visit until he died.

PART V

THE EXILE—
"TUSITALA"

SHELLEY ROSE

EXHIBITIONS INCLUDE ROBERT LOUIS STEVENSON & AUS-
TRALASIA FOR COMMONWEALTH FESTIVAL (EDINBURGH) &
FORTHCOMING SARA ALLGOOD — DOWN UNDER DUBLIN

BORN: SYDNEY, AUSTRALIA · EXHIBITION RESEARCHER

STEVENSON
IN AUSTRALASIA

STEVENSON IN AUSTRALASIA

SHELLEY ROSE

When the children are playing alone on the green,
In comes the playmate that never was seen.
When children are happy and lonely and good,
The Friend of the Children comes out of the wood.

Nobody heard him and nobody saw,
His is a picture you never could draw,
But he is sure to be present, abroad or at home,
When children are happy and playing alone.
   THE UNSEEN PLAYMATE.
   A CHILD'S GARDEN OF VERSES

The pleasures of childhood are easily recalled when I remember my father purchasing 'The Golden Pathway' —a set of blue volumes of 'romance' — with which he lovingly introduced me to the world of literature. Brimful of hours of learning and delight via the music of words and images, the first volume had an illustration of a serene-faced woman leading a donkey with child astride through a wood, beneath which was the quotation:
   'The world is so full of a number of things,
   I'm sure we should all be as happy as kings.'
   It echoed an optimism toward life and thus Robert Louis Stevenson settled into my mind and became the preface to my childhood. Amongst nursery rhymes and familiar bed-time stories was a favourite colour-plate of a citadelled castle surrounded by a steep, spiralled pathway. Several decades later I found myself travelling to a similarly precipitous, castled place which was the birthplace of the writer.
   By the age of seven I had graduated to other books which 'excite or console' and these included *Treasure Island*, and *Kidnapped*, where I sensed the uselessness of hiding from Blind Pew as he tenaciously tapped his way to the Admiral

Benbow Inn and catapulted Jim Hawkins into a miasma of greed and adventure; likewise I sympathised with the brave David Balfour as he battled with political treachery. Long before critical judgement is formed, the moral see-saw of good and evil is visible to tender eyes.

Graham Greene in his essay 'The Lost Childhood' wrote of the gratitude we owe to those writers who stimulate our early imagination, whose very names cause a 'missed heart-beat', for as he wrote: 'in childhood all books are books of divinations, telling us about the future and as such they become beacons to our inner lives.'

I have long been fascinated by those who leave the status quo and venture into the wider world — such journeys are manifestations of man's eternal spiritual quest — and this lured me to books about travellers in the Pacific where I chanced upon a copy of Stevenson's *In the South Seas*. Here was the mature Stevenson and although the charm and cadence of his prose was more polished, the same quixotic vein of adventure remained.

I was drawn by Stevenson's poignant portrayal of the struggles of the indigenous South Sea Islanders against those who sought to convert, exploit and conquer them. Stevenson found new creative stimulus in their rich oral tradition and revelled in having *escaped the shadow of the Roman Empire* and with the improvement in his fragile health, he renounced his northern habitat to *spend his days in fairyland* in Samoa; which he instantly recognised as the typography of his favourite childhood book, RM Ballantyne's 'Coral Island'.

My appetite whetted, I read more of Stevenson's Pacific opus: *Island Nights' Entertainments* (born out of his third Pacific cruise aboard the 'Janet Nicholl'), *The Wrecker* (part of which was set in Sydney), *Footnote to History, The Ebb-Tide, Vailima Letters* and the lesser known works which mirror the fine-fibred nature of the man: 'Father Damien Letter, Missions in the South Seas' and 'An Object of Pity'. Reading of the link these had with Sydney, my hometown, questions arose in my mind as to what Sydney's profile was like then. The beautiful harbour remains the same today, with its honeycombed bays, though the tall-masted ships are gone as are the Georgian and Victorian buildings which so reminded Stevenson of Paris and London. Where did he stay and whom did he meet? Such ponderables encouraged me to research his four Sydney sojourns between 1890 and 1893, and I accumulated a quantity of undiscovered material.

I conducted the bulk of this research at the Mitchell Library in Sydney which has a formidable collection of works relating to Australasia and the Pacific. Stevenson had himself heard of this valuable library and had once called upon the reticent Scottish bibliophile David Scott Mitchell — unfortunately the latter considered Stevenson too bohemian to entertain!

The rich spectrum of pictorial material I discovered convinced me an exhibition was necessary and I was keen to share it with those who knew something of Stevenson's background. What better place than his hometown of 'Auld Reekie'. I contacted the Edinburgh Central Library with its large Stevenson collection (especially relating to his Pacific voyages) and I was delighted with their enthusiastic response and help in promoting my plans for exhibition. Out of this dialogue came the more comprehensive plan: 'RLS '86' as part of the Edinburgh Festival, that annual smörgasbord of worldwide artistic endeavour.

The desire to follow the tangible footsteps of Stevenson seems to arise in many who study his life and works; somehow his spirit possesses a quality of the Pied Piper to those who leave their 'hills of home'. The choice of direction is wide, for Stevenson traversed two hemispheres, yet for the more timorous armchair traveller there is a plethora of books covering his infinite trails — RLS has been conveniently dovetailed into twentieth century tourism!

Poised to leave Sydney to follow my own Stevenson trail, one night I dreamt I saw Stevenson on television. Magnificent obsessions are all very well, but I felt this was invading my psyche too much! Richard Holmes in his book 'Footsteps' aptly described this quality of being 'haunted' by one's subject. Several days later however I was amazed to receive a telephone call from the Australian Broadcasting Corporation.

They were making a mini-series for television about Stevenson's life in Samoa, to be called 'Tusitala'. They had heard of my research and wanted to view material for costume design purposes.

Eventually I departed for Scotland and decided to punctuate my long flight across the Pacific by visiting places where Stevenson had been. I began in Auckland where one of his Balfour relatives had designed many of the lighthouses along the N.Z. coastline for Stevenson had visited several of them. Then on to Hawaii to research at the exotic Bishop Museum in Honolulu, where the Polynesian culture is so evident. I also toured the lovely island of Molokai, scene of the Father Damien episode in Stevenson's life. Somewhat jet-lagged I continued to Los Angeles where I made my way to the Huntington Museum (one of the greatest collections of art and literature in the world), followed by a quick sojourn in the lush Napa Valley to see the Silverado Museum. Next to New York and the New York Public Library, constantly winnowing what was relevant. Finally I flew to London (where I had lived a decade earlier), with familiar haunts to be revisited in between forays to the British Museum, the Mansell Collection, the National Portrait Gallery and the BBC's Radio Times Hulton Picture Library. Stevenson material is as scattered as Stevenson trails, its by-ways as numerous.

At last I arrived in Edinburgh, weighed down with my papery endeavours. I was warmly welcomed by the staff of the Central Library and soon felt at home. Edinburgh is a jewelled city who wears her history with a dazzling confidence. Wherever one turns, there is another aspect of her past to consider — no wonder she has sired such fine talent. Often during my preparations for the exhibition, I would look out of the Library window and there would be Edinburgh Castle, perched high above on a craggy granite seat. With the Commonwealth Games to be held in Edinburgh that July, and a part of which was to be a Festival uniting the various participating countries, it was decided to schedule ·my opening to include that event, since many Australian and New Zealand travellers to Edinburgh would then be able to enjoy images of

Stevenson in their own terrain, learning how he viewed their homeland.

'R.L.S. '86' proved a proper celebration of the life and work of Stevenson. Coinciding with the centenary of the publication of *Kidnapped* and *Dr Jekyll & Mr Hyde,* this was the first major festival about this great son of Scotland held in Edinburgh: suddenly during that summer, Stevenson was upon everyone's lips. I was amazed at the foreign visitors who toured my exhibition and who spoke fondly of the sacred place Stevenson held for them. There was an 'Inaugural Stevenson Supper' held at Stevenson's local Swanston pub, The Hunter's Tryst. The chosen dishes came complete with corresponding literary quotes and ranged from 'Long John Silver's F'o'sle Broth' through to 'Coffee from the Indies' capped off with 'Cap'n Flint's Mints', while a strong 'Pirate Punch' helped the conviviality. Stevenson, who had been a great lover of such feasts, would have relished such a scene in his honour.

With the ball over and the glitter and the guests vanished, Edinburgh wore her more sedate face. I travelled on to Ireland in early 1987, displaying an edited version of 'Robert Louis Stevenson and Australasia' at the famous Abbey Theatre in Dublin to those smiling-eyed Irish. There was an intense interest in Stevenson's spirited defence of the Catholic 'leper' priest Father Damien, of whose heroic life of sacrifice the Irish were well aware. As in Edinburgh, I made friends and was able to taste another experience and learn more of these islands from which we in the far flung south are historically descended, and towards whom we feel such strong cultural ties.

Eventually the sun, my family and friends called me southward, so I returned to Australia feeling that I had fulfilled my initial purpose in showing the more mature Stevenson — his ties during his Pacific years with my own country — to northerners who may never see these 'beautiful places, green for ever; perfect climate', where time relaxes so there is 'nothing to do but study oratory and etiquette, sit in the sun and pick up the fruits as they fall.'

R J Storey

WORKED IN SCANDINAVIA, WESTERN ISLES AND SHETLAND BEFORE JOINING STAFF OF HIGHLANDS AND ISLANDS DEVELOPMENT BOARD

BORN INDIA · READ ENGLISH AND HISTORY AT GLASGOW UNIV & ANTHROPOLOGY AT OXFORD · MA (GLASGOW) · WRITTEN AND BROADCAST ON VARIOUS ISLAND TOPICS

Serendipity & St Ives

SERENDIPITY & ST IVES

RJ STOREY

*The right kind of thing should fall out in the right kind
of place; the right kind of thing should follow; and not
only the characters talk aptly and think naturally, but
all the circumstances in a tale answer one to another
like notes in music. The threads of a story come from
time to time together and make a picture in the web; the
characters fall from time to time into some attitude to
each other or to nature, which stamps the story home
like an illustration.*

A GOSSIP ON ROMANCE

Until I bought *Vailima Letters* on impulse one day at a sec-
ond-hand book stall, I knew little of Stevenson's work. The
man himself was more familiar. I had heard much about him
from my grandfather, a contemporary who could recall the
effect when news of his death reached Scotland from Samoa.

Vailima Letters immediately appealed, but contained a puzzle. In a letter dated 30 January, 1893, Stevenson listed tenta-
tive chapter titles for his new novel *St Ives,* about the fortunes
of a French prisoner-of-war who escapes from Edinburgh
Castle. Almost at the end of the list is a chapter headed 'The
True Blooded Yankee', immediately preceding one which indicates the hero's return to France.

The 'True Blooded Yankee' was a name I recognised as the
most formidable of the American vessels that preyed on
British coastal shipping in the War of 1812-14. These opera-
tions are little known, and I had been prompted to undertake
spare time research, over more years that I care to admit, on
an unsupported statement in an American source that the
'True Blooded Yankee' had 'captured a town in Scotland'.

The claim proved not far from the truth, and other incidents were scarcely less arresting. Most involved privateers — fast, well-armed vessels owned by civilians but licensed by government to take or destroy British ships.

Was Stevenson referring to 'The True Blooded Yankee' I knew, and did he mean to use her in the escape of St Ives as the chapter headings suggested? Certainly she would have been appropriate. The Americans were allies of France, and the ship was active on the Scottish coast at the time in question. Her most daring raid would have well suited Stevenson's purpose and powers.

But RLS had died before completing the novel, and Arthur Quiller-Couch, widely known as 'Q', had been commissioned to write the conclusion. Advice on Stevenson's intentions was provided by his step-daughter, Belle Strong, to whom much of the book had been dictated. I turned to 'Q's ending and found no reference to 'The True Blooded Yankee'. There was instead a turn of plot which took St Ives to France by way, not of Scottish waters, but the coast of Cornwall, where 'Q' had his own home. The whole business of the escape was strangely convoluted and, I felt, unconvincing.

I found reassurance on Stevenson's intentions elsewhere in *Vailima Letters*. In a postscript he asks an American friend, *'Were all your privateers voiceless in the War of 1812? Did no one of them write memoirs?'* An editorial footnote confirms that the query relates to the involvement of an American privateer in the rescue of St. Ives.

The Beinecke Library at Yale provided further evidence, with notes on *St Ives* in Stevenson's own hand and that of Belle Strong. Even more telling were letters held at Princeton. In these Quiller-Couch refers to his difficulties with the escape of St Ives, which stemmed largely from his refusal to believe that American privateers would have operated in British waters. He expresses 'horror and dismay' on discovering his error too late.

In a foreword to the new edition of *St Ives,* I present this and other material more fully, with an account of 'The True Blooded Yankee's' most colourful exploit — the episode which forms the cornerstone of Jenni Calder's new ending and which had aroused my original interest in the privateer. This incident may well have brought the ship to Stevenson's attention, conceivably in material sent out to Samoa, or just as possibly through an account passed on by one of his light-house building forebears. (His grandfather — in company with Sir Walter Scott — had been at risk of capture by an American vessel.) Whatever the case, Stevenson knew enough to recognise the attraction of 'The True Blooded Yankee', but the query I have referred to, and another to his American publisher, make it clear that he wanted the human detail — *'the facts and faces'*, as he put it — that would bring her to life. It would probably not have surprised him that what he sought was even then to be found, vivid and original, in Scotland.

Astonishingly, it was still there when I had reason to search for it myself. 'The True Blooded Yankee's' capture of a Scottish town had proved to be a raid on the harbour of Bowmore, on the island of Islay, in December, 1813. I had come across an account of this episode in a letter written by an eye-witness, a young exciseman. He described the raid in graphic detail, from the capture of two islanders who offered to pilot the vessel, to the burning of shipping in the harbour after threats to destroy the town had sent women and children into the hills. I decided to visit the island in the slender hope that some memory of the affair might remain.

I remember well the night of my arrival on Islay, a witching-ly beautiful island. I was staying at an hotel in Bowmore, close to the harbour raided by the privateer, and on mention-ing my interest in local history I was directed to a retired sea captain sitting a few feet away in the lounge bar. The response to my question was emphatic. Yes, there had been a raid. Ships had been burned at Bowmore. Then, referring to the master of the American vessel, he riveted my attention with the words, 'We call him the Bloody Yankee'. The link with 'The True Blooded Yankee' seemed suddenly very real, but he could tell me little more with certainty. He gave me names of other islanders who knew of the affair, including one Gilbert Clark of Port Charlotte.

Over the next few days I heard the story of 'The Bloody Yankee' several times, in English and in Gaelic. (I was greatly favoured in having with me a Gaelic speaker, now my wife.) Despite a confusion with John Paul Jones, who had been dead for over 20 years at the time of the raid, these narratives were impressively consistent with the exciseman's letter. Most strikingly, they had the classic features of oral tradition — freshness in the telling, the characteristics of local people and places, and perhaps above all the recollection of words used at the time. The scene on the deck of the privateer, and the exchanges between the captured Islay pilot and the American crew (including a warning from a Gaelic-speaking privateersman when the pilot tried to run the ship aground), were described to me as though they had taken place the previous week.

Gilbert Clark of Port Charlotte proved to be a man with whom Stevenson would have had ready rapport. A vigorous 60-year old joiner and boat-builder, he had a vast knowledge of island history, and an infectious enthusiasm. His respect for the past and the need for its faithful recording marked him as a natural scholar. He took me to places significant in the raid and to descendants of people involved. We visited the ruins of the mill operated by Neil Connell, the captured Islay pilot, and looked out on the entrance to Loch Indaal, up which 'The True Blooded Yankee' had sailed in 'the Year of the Burned Ships', as it became known in Gaelic. On her way back to sea, he told me, the privateer had bombarded the shore of the loch, and two of her cannon-balls were used in shot-putting contests at local games until well into the present century.

Undoubtedly Stevenson had chosen a device for the escape of St Ives that was both colourful and authentic. Yet however much he knew of the Islay background, a crucial question poses itself. How was his hero to reach the island from Edinburgh to make his transfer to the privateer? The solution lies again in Stevenson's own notes and in the advice of Belle Strong. St Ives was to take advantage of a public demonstration of balloon flight — a fashionable diversion of the time —

to escape from hot pursuit in the Pentlands, surely one of the earliest deliverances by air in fiction. Quiller-Couch chose to send the balloon the length of Britain to his own home territory, but Stevenson's papers make it clear that England was not the destination planned. In a list of chapter headings held at Yale, 'The Balloon Ascension' is followed immediately by 'The East Wind Blows'. Due west of the balloon's point of departure lies the Island of Islay.

Other commitments forced me to let 'The True Blooded Yankee' rest for a number of years, though in that time I was able to reduce my ignorance of Stevenson's work and to appreciate the range of his talent. I have explained that I knew something of his remarkable life, but I had not previously related this to the writing; and now the process exerted its predictably compelling effect. Biographers were of course helpful at the complex levels — Furnas and Calder especially so — but at root the fascination lay largely for me, as for so many, in the more patent features of his exile in Samoa, and their expression or repression in his work.

Clearly *St Ives* was not one of his greater novels, and the literary world seemed unlikely to halt in its rotation if Quiller-Couch's conclusion were to stand. Yet Stevenson's intention for the ending reflected much of his own character and affinities: the colour and dash of the raid, the appeal of sea, ships and islands — all in an unmistakably Scottish setting. Opportunity for redress seemed unlikely but a sense of obligation to Stevenson remained.

I was resigned to producing little more about *St Ives* than an aside in a paper on privateering when I heard that a film (not the first) was to be made of the book. It seemed that the plot was to be freely interpreted and 'a heightened level of humour' introduced. The project ran into difficulties, but it confirmed the need for a version of the book which would do the fullest possible justice to the author's intentions. Interestingly, the film company had noted that the denouement could provide a problem.

It was about this time that the Glasgow publisher, Richard Drew, sought to identify work by Stevenson for republication, and turned for advice to Jenni Calder, author of 'RLS: A Life Study', and much else. I knew nothing of this, but by the kind of fortuity that would have appealed to Stevenson, had arranged to lunch with Jenni Calder to discuss the matter of St Ives and 'The True Blooded Yankee'. The outcome was a proposal to Richard Drew for a new edition of *St Ives*, with a completely revised conclusion. To reproduce Stevenson's style was beyond my powers, but it was a task for which Jenni Calder was pre-eminently suited. Richard Drew, a publisher of flair, agreed.

Jenni Calder went to Islay herself in due course, and absorbed what people and places there had to convey. Her handling of the conclusion is clearly informed by her visit, and complements her fine treatment of earlier scenes in and around Edinburgh. She was involved by this time in two other Stevenson publications, and pressure on her was acute when I was told of a Glasgow academic, Alastair Wardlaw, who was a direct descendant of the miller captured by 'The True Blooded Yankee'. Prof. Wardlaw had compiled a meticulous family history, including details of the miller's appearance still known on Islay but missed by me. As deadlines closed, Jenni Calder took pains to change her text and incorporate the material. It is this concern for 'facts and faces', no less than her skeely evocation of Stevenson's style, that suggests justice has been done to the author of *St Ives*.

Jenni Calder

BORN: CHICAGO · TAUGHT/ LECTURED: SCOTLAND, ENGLAND, ITALY, KENYA AND USA · BA MPHIL (CANTAB). WORKS FOR NATIONAL MUSEUMS OF SCOTLAND, EDINBURGH.

EDITED DR JEKYLL AND MR HYDE, KIDNAPPED, CATRIONA AND RE-WRITTEN ENDING OF ST IVES · BOOKS INCLUDE RLS — A LIFE STUDY AND ROBERT LOUIS STEVENSON COMPANION, ROBERT LOUIS STEVENSON & VICTORIAN SCOTLAND

Balloons &
Other Inventions

BALLOONS & OTHER INVENTIONS
JENNI CALDER

*I can write no more just now, and I hope you will be
able to decipher so much, for it contains matter. Really,
the whole of yesterday's work would do in a novel without one bit of embellishment; and, indeed, few novels
are so amusing. Bough, Miss Amy, Mrs Ross, Blackie,
M— the parson — all these were such distinct characters, the incidents were so entertaining, and the scenery
so fine, that the whole would have made a novelist's fortune.*

FROM A LETTER, EARRAID,

THURSDAY, AUGUST 5TH 1870

I was on the Island of Islay, on the trail of a ship called 'The
True Blooded Yankee', a fictional balloon flight and an invent-
ed hero. I had come to the island guided by Bob Storey and
his researches into Stevenson's intriguing mention in connection with his novel *St Ives* of an American privateer in Scottish
water. I was spending most of my time getting the feel of the
place. I paced out the broad main street of Bowmore, from
the distillery to the harbour, up to the round church which
offered no corners to hide the devil. I tramped the shore by
Kintra Farm, where Mrs MacTaggart made me wonderfully
comfortable, and looked across at the wide entrance to Loch
Indaal. I took the shore road to Bruichladdich and Port
Charlotte and found the site of an old mill and medieval grave
slabs. They would both prove very much to the purpose.

I had in my mind a ship slipping quietly up the loch in darkness. A balloon ascending from the slopes of the Pentlands
near Edinburgh, blown due west across the Clyde estuary and

Kintyre, and coming down where Loch Indaal opens into the sea. The more time I spent in Islay the more convinced I was that Stevenson would have relished not only the idea of bringing the hero of his escape story together with a marauding privateer that fired ships in the Bowmore anchorage, but the place itself. For it offered everything that Stevenson responded to most strongly: a small green island, a vast expanse of grey ocean, a powerfully surviving past which had not only kept alive the tale of the raiding Yankee but reached much further back, as is evidenced by the quivering, translucent, ghostly aura of Finlaggan, ancient centre of the Lords of the Isles.

I was not attempting to impersonate Stevenson, but I had taken on a challenging task — to finish his novel *St Ives* which he had been working on up to near the time of his death on 3 December 1894. Shortly after this Arthur Quiller-Couch had taken on with gusto and in haste the job of supplying the missing chapters. The result was six chapters which tell us a great deal about the appeal of Stevenson in the late nineteenth century. There was a climate of reaction against middle-class domestic fiction. There was an appetite for quirky romance and spirited adventure, and in responding to this Stevenson recognized the scope for experiment. Quiller-Couch took this up and pushed it further, perhaps, than Stevenson would have done, for however much 'Q' admired Stevenson he was not in touch with the historical and moral foundations on which he built. *St Ives* is not a 'serious' historical novel, like *The Master of Ballantrae* or *Weir of Hermiston*, but it could not have been written without Stevenson's profound sense of Scotland's past and the ambiguities of Scotland's moralities. 'Q' did not share this sense and it is understandable that he took St Ives out of Scotland as quickly as he decently could. I felt that Stevenson would have intended Scotland to feature more strongly in the novel's denouement.

It would not have occurred to me to attempt a different ending for *St Ives* if Bob Storey's researches had not pointed to such tantalizing and convincing possibilities. Was it really likely that Stevenson had planned something rather different and more historically based than 'Q's' bizarre convergence of coincidences? It seemed to me it was. To take that on board intellectually was one thing. To act on that understanding was something else. I read and re-read the novel. I climbed Caerketton above Swanston, the Stevenson's family summer home which is a key player in *St Ives*, and mapped out the movements of St Ives and Flora, and the chase across the Pentland slopes. I located a spot in a fold of the hills near the Hunter's Tryst where I reckoned a gas balloon could take to the air. I resolved to make use of my own home ground, South Queensferry, which Stevenson had visited often. Although there was nothing to suggest he had any such intention, it seemed appropriate and it felt right.

And in the end that's what it came down to. I rewrote the last chapters of *St Ives* on the basis partly of the meticulous research made available to me by Bob Storey, partly on the basis of what felt right. If the results of the research had *not* felt right, I could not have done it. Nor could I have attempted it if I had not been sure of my localities. But most of all I could not have even begun to think about adding to a work by Stevenson if I had not spent years studying both his life and his work, because without that I could not have developed any kind of instinct for what would work and what belonged.

The task was influenced by my understanding of Stevenson — that I recognized at the outset. What I had not anticipated was the way my understanding of Stevenson was influenced by the task. I made no attempt to get inside the skull of the author I was imitating: that would have been fruitless and misleading. I immersed myself in his style and concentrated on fine-tuning my sense of what was fitting. I tried to be inventive without being extravagant. It was an attempt at a double illusion, to recreate a late nineteenth-century piece of fiction which was itself recreating an early nineteenth-century sensibility. What readers have access to now is a late twentieth-century interpretation which may perhaps prove to be as revealing of current attitudes to Stevenson as Quiller-Couch's rendering is of another generation's.

I enjoyed the writing as much as anything I've ever done —

perhaps more. And through that enjoyment I understood better than before Stevenson's own pleasure in setting free the imagination. There was a vivid anarchic streak in his make-up, which we can detect best in his letters and in some of his tales of his exploits, exploits that he was as likely to indulge in at forty as he was at twenty. We knew he was often driven by a quest for adventure. This was much more than a search for thrills — it was a striving to reach beyond the expected, the controlled, the circumscribed. *'Life is far better fun than people dream who fall asleep among the chimney stacks and telegraph wires,'* as he wrote to his rather staid and stay-at-home friend Sidney Colvin. Yet he had been brought up to understand the need for control, for constraint, and he never un-learned that lesson. This is the central, and immensely rewarding, tension of his work, as strong in *St Ives,* though not one of his best books, as in almost everything else he wrote. The book is most rewarding when the fanciful is hand-in-hand with the real, when comedy is enacted in the vivid streets of a living city, or a balloon soars above the contours of known mountains.

The pleasure I derive from reading Stevenson has a great deal to do with that tension: invalid and adventurer, moralist and anarchist, realist and romancer, David Balfour and Alan Breck, Edinburgh and the South Seas. It appealed to me when I first read him with real attention, when I was working on a book on heroes, and each time I go back to him fresh aspects of this edgy, creative, polarity emerge. It has often been described in terms of a dualism intrinsic to Scotland's history and character, but I think it is much more than that. It is part of an end-of-a-century, end-of-an-era restlessness, which, a century later, perhaps strikes a particular chord.

In most of his work Stevenson uses irony to handle and manipulate that tension — subtle, often affectionate, sometimes quite savage, but always the pivot by which he turns to the light different facets of his characters and their dilemmas of action and morality. It is present in *St Ives* and catching that self-conscious, almost self-mocking tone of the first-person narrative was part of the challenge. Stevenson himself had played the '*sedulous ape*': I took my cue from him. But a single wrong word or reference or even comma could ruin the illusion, and I am much indebted to those who read the type-script and drew attention to infelicities. But on occasion it is possible that Stevenson himself got it wrong. Would St Ives have drunk claret in 1813, or 'wine of Bordeaux'? Stevenson had him drinking claret, so I stayed with that, although it may be an anachronism.

There are different kinds of authenticity. Stevenson was very sensitive to place. It was essential not only literally to fol-low in his footsteps, but to achieve some understanding of the way he responded. On his beloved Pentlands that wasn't too difficult. He himself had written so much about the 'hills of home'. But on Islay there was nothing to go on, although he may have been there during a lighthouse-inspection trip with his father or when he later cruised the Inner Hebrides with his friend Walter Simpson. And even on the shore between Cramond and Queensferry, my only help lay in *Kidnapped* and occasional mentions elsewhere. But these were locations that I was confident Stevenson could and would have made much of. He would have absorbed and used them with loving accuracy. I tried to do the same. In ending *St Ives* at Queensferry's Hawes Inn I was in a sense 'quoting' from *Kidnapped,* but I was also drawing on my experience as well as his, and reminding myself, if not my readers, that writing those final chapters was a tribute, not an appropriation.

James S Winegar

RUNS HIS OWN FIRM IN PROVO, UTAH · ACTIVE IN DOWNS SYNDROME SOCIETY, U.S. AND PRESIDENT OF R.L.S. RESTORATION & PRESERVATION SOCIETY

ATTENDED BRIGHAM YOUNG UNIVERSITY, UTAH · MISSIONARY TO WESTERN SAMOA IN APIA, IS NOW TEACHER

Stevensonomania —Why the Passion?

STEVENSONOMANIA— WHY THE PASSION?

JAMES WINEGAR

Let now your soul in this substantial world
Some anchor strike. Be here the body moored —
This spectacle immutably from now
The picture in your eye; and when time strikes,
And the green scene goes on the instant blind —
The ultimate helpers, where your horse today
Conveyed you dreaming, bear your body dead.

AN END OF TRAVEL.

SONGS OF TRAVEL (VAILIMA)

My relationship with RLS began in curiosity after having seen his Samoa home at Vailima many years ago. It was the home of the New Zealand High Commissioner, for it was associated, as it still is, as a residence for high government officials rather than the home built by RLS. As an appointee, the commissioner's primary function is that of colonial overlord on this group of relatively small islands known as Samoa that appear on maps as almost indistinguishable dots. Enquiring locally I could find virtually no one who could tell me anything about the RLS connection, other than that he came from Scotland and was a writer

Conversation today with almost any middle-aged, middle-class Samoan might reveal something like this:

'What's behind those concrete pillars and the gates on the right side of the Vailima Road about three miles up?'

'Oh, that's the Government House.'

'Who lives there?'

'You mean now?'

'Yes, now, but also in the past?'

'Well, it's the home of the head-of-state, but as long as I can remember, government officials have lived there.'

'Okay, but who built the house?'

'Tusitala, he built the house a long time ago and lived in it until he died. My people loved him and they carried his body to the top of the mountain above the house to be buried.'

'Who was Tusitala?'

'He was a writer. His Scottish surname is difficult for Samoans to pronounce so he was named Tusitala because he wrote stories.'

'What did he write?'

'He wrote the poem on his tombstone.'

The discovery that virtually no one in Samoa knew or appreciated RLS shocked me. Through no fault of their own, these people have escaped the passion and intensity which surround the life and writing of their most famous citizen.

The sincere interest (shared by my close associates) to do something which benefited all of Samoa focussed on a mission to restore and preserve the home and grave of RLS. In preparing to make this commitment and in order to gain the confidence of the local government, I had to investigate the life of RLS but with necessary emphasis on the Samoa years. In doing so, I have become incurably smitten with the history and I can identify with the character and his supporting cast, particularly when they were on location at Vailima. What began for me as a cursory look into the life of RLS has evolved into a passion.

Once a curiosity about Louis and his close associates is aroused, there is no lack of resources and reference material. Researchers, scholars and biographers often bask in the challenge of finding something out of nothing — they dig through scanty amounts of 'hard' information for clues and hints — to authenticate dates and events and elusive personal detail. But this is hardly the case with RLS. His life is one of the most widely documented during the period in which he lived. Why so? Probably because he was such a faithful friend to those he loved. He was a compulsive communicator — whether writ-

ing or verbally, he was constantly searching for seeds of ideas
and planting passionate opinions on a vast variety of subjects.

He created a standard of personal letter writing that possibly remains unchallenged today, for it seems no matter who
wrote to him, they were almost assured that they would
receive an answer. As a result, a faithful following constantly
petitioned advice from his sage counsel — his replies are
replete with solid recommendations for achieving the most
out of love, occupation, education and relationships.

What is the genesis of this passion? Is it the man himself
and his free approach to life, or is it his vast number of relationships with truly unique characters? Could it be a fascination with the places he went, the things he did, or does it lie
in his writings and the development of his personal philosophy? Might it be the adventure that he encountered in over-
coming adversities of health, or is to capture the quality of the
'little boy' in me who wishes still to hear the meter and envi-
sion the fantasy of going to sleep every night to *A Child's
Garden of Verses* read by a loving mother?

His own passion is infectious and his personal internaliza-
tion admirable. When he wrote to George Meredith that he
could not remember a time when he hadn't awakened sick
nor gone to bed weary, he said '*I have written in bed, and written
out of it, written in haemorrhages, written in sickness, written torn by
coughing, written when my head swam for weakness. I was made for a con-
test, and the Powers have so willed that my battlefield be this dingy bed,*'.
He spent nearly all his life in '*expectation of death*', yet throughout it he did what he did as if it were the only thing in the
world that was worth being done. Passion indeed.

The pen and writing table were his medium. He became
extremely skilled at expressing his opinions, many of which
were adopted by those less eloquent in their abilities to
express their own feelings. Whilst reading his letters to his
old cronies it is easy for me to slip into fantasy about his talent
— it is as though he had me in mind when he wrote them.
Incidents and anecdotes about the way his writings have
touched other lives are legion, they are usually extremely personal but become an intimate part of a wider fabric of passion.

RLS certainly had his share of personal challenges to overcome which taxed his physical, mental and spiritual being.
When those challenges are put into perspective, one cannot
escape the profound respect for what he made of himself. He
was for instance an only child, born to proud doting parents
who had preconceived notions as to who and what he would
become. He was born with gifts of the sensitive and a keen
intellect that caused him to question authority, regardless of
its source. Though physically weak and frail throughout his
life his vivid imagination and fantasies drove him on. His
rebelliousness caused him problems that could have easily
been avoided had he conformed. In courting older women,
and eventually marrying one, he went against the grain of the
social mores of the time. A strong spirit of adventure was
played-out in the South Seas which provided him, as it still
does for anyone today, a veritable cornucopia of vicarious
experience for those who attempt it. Eventually returning to
his family to appease his parents he never compromised his
own values. Constant presence of death meant living bravely
and to the fullest. A love for the simple people of Samoa
meant integrating into their way of life with its contrast to
European religion, prayer, politics and personal relationships.

I believe that Louis would have been very comfortable in
the climate of Berkeley, in the early 1970's; for while he was
from an aristocratic background, he didn't go along with the
accepted lifestyle and the expectations of the day, so that
although he enjoyed the finer privileges he was quite willing
to point-out injustices and class distinction. His treatment of
women and their rights was totally contrary to the chauvinistic
attitudes of his day — attitudes that still exists to some degree
today.

The RLS passion becomes a very possessive pursuit, so that
being thrust into the mainstream of today's social life, I am
afforded the opportunity of meeting the contemporary equiva-
lents to the Colvins, Henleys, Baxters, Osbournes, Strongs,
Balfours, Moors and so forth. The unique characters of today
are known to me by the names of Wakefield, Maugham,
Nielson (involved with Vailima restoration); of Strouse,

Furnas, Daiches, Calder, Mehew, to say nothing of Shaffer, VanDyke, Warfel and Knight and countless unnamed others. The preservation of the memory and passion of RLS is in good hands.

The restoration of Stevenson's Vailima home as an international treasure is yet another expression of his enduring passion. It might even provide the motivation for Samoans to learn and appreciate who Louis was and what he did for them. Then they will discover the fire and passion of his life and possibly will add their names to the list of those who can say they believe RLS continues to contribute to the quality of their lives.

FAY ALA'ILMA

BIOGRAPHY OF AGGIE GREY (SAMOAN HOTEL-KEEPER) AND MY SAMOAN CHIEF · LIVES IN APIA WITH HER HUSBAND, WHO IS UNDER SECRETARY TO PRIME MINISTER OF SAMOA, AND THEIR SIX CHILDREN

BORN: 1921, NEW YORK STATE · STUDIED: OHIO · WORKED WITH POLISH REFUGEES IN QUAKER PROGRAM & UNITED NATIONS TEAM IN AUSTRIA

WHY SAMOANS REMEMBER TUSITALA

WHY SAMOANS REMEMBER TUSITALA

FAY ALA'ILMA

Now we were to return, like the voyager in the play, and see what rearrangements fortune had perfected the while in our surroundings; what surprises stood ready made for us at home; and whither and how far the world had voyaged in our absence. You may paddle all day long; but it is when you come back at nightfall, and look in at the familiar room, that you will find Love, or Death awaiting beside the stove; and the most beautiful adventures are not those we go to seek.

AN INLAND VOYAGE

Many 'palagis' (Europeans) have come to our islands in the past 100 years: royals, governors, colonels, high commissioners, missionaries, movie actors and millionaires. Why is it that the only name universally remembered is 'Tusitala' (Teller of Tales) the title we gave an emaciated young Scotchman who was here off and on for only five years between 1889 and 1894.

Is it because of his wondrous mansion still gracing the hills above Apia? Governors, High Commissioners and our own Head of State have lived there since but we still call it 'Robert Louis Stevenson's place'. Is it because he is buried on top of Mt Vaea nearby? Tourists are more apt to scramble up there than Samoans. Why take chances? 'Aitu' (ghosts) could be flitting around that dark forest, just as he warned. But we all know the words on his grave by heart nonetheless. Our teachers put them to music and every schoolchild sings that song.

Is it because we have all read his poems and stories? I

doubt it. No Samoan mother I know recites poems to her children from *A Child's Garden of Verses*. If she did she might be hard pressed to explain '*In winter I get up at night*' and railway carriages that are '*Faster than fairies, faster than witches.*' Samoan adolescents would doubtless thrill to *Treasure Island* and *Kidnapped* but struggling with English would spoil the fun.

It is possible that the things we love in Tusitala are not his books but the very qualities that used to set European teeth on edge about him. Let me give a few examples.

My husband's family comes from the small island of Manono which gives its traditional allegiance to High Chief Malietoa. In 1889 there was some dissention on the island due to the fact that there were two Malietoas. Most families favoured one called Mata'afa and the village council fore-stalled potential fighting by telling the pro-Laupepa family to move elsewhere. That is a traditional way to keep harmony in a Samoan community, but apparently displeased the German Chief Justice in Apia (a Laupepa man himself), who sent a war-ship to our island, seized five of our Mata'afa chiefs, and threw them in jail in Apia, saying he did not approve of barbaric cus-toms like 'banishment'. When we tried to rescue our leaders, he resorted to the practice himself however, and had them deported to the Marshalls for safe-keeping. Only one European understood our feeling of injustice and helpless-ness. Tusitala wrote to the London *Times* in an effort to get them back — a fact that did not endear him to most of the white community but made him a hero with us.

When war broke out in 1893 the three consuls also ban-ished Mata'afa himself. Tusitala remembered his supporters thrown into the Apia jail without enough to eat. He not only sent food but came down to party with them himself — the sign of a true ally. They reciprocated by clearing the road to his house still called the 'Ala o le Alofa' (Road of the Loving Heart).

Does Manono still recall their champion of a hundred years ago, even with benefit of the history books? In 1987 when my husband was running for Parliament for that district, the chiefs of Manono often spent the night with us, not to sound out his platform but to watch his video. We decided to feature a 6-part mini-series on the life of Tusitala, wondering if they could follow it in English. No problem. The domestic scenes may have escaped them but not the political rallies at Mata'afa's village, played by Samoans speaking in Samoan. The effect was electric. They stayed up all night astonished and excited, trying to locate the faces of their grandfathers in the crowd. Most thought it was really Mata'afa and came back night after night with their friends. My husband figures he owes that election to Tusitala.

I often wondered how Robert Louis Stevenson, disembarking from a yacht into a tight little white enclave like Apia, ever got to meet Mata'afa who certainly did not frequent that social circle. The answer occurred to me one evening in 1960 when we were having tea with 'Uncle Harry' at his home in Ululoloa. The walls were covered with pictures of his father, old H J Moors (HJM), partying with Robert Louis Stevenson. Harry explained that HJM was a man of many parts into all sorts of things. In 1875 he had jumped an American ship with only a bale of onions and a chest of cloth and set up a bush store in Savaii, with copra as a medium of exchange. Two years later he had mastered the language, made a profit, and was back in Apia as a partner of an old German shyster named Grevsmuhl. Experience soon taught him he would never hit it off with missionaries, consuls, or German traders, so he built his own store farther up the waterfront and set out to find more congenial companions. He soon did. One was with 'Nimo' a dark-eyed Samoan beauty whom he married forthwith. Like most Samoans she was a fan of Mata'afa and soon arranged for her husband to meet him. The relationship was so congenial — and profitable as well. They found they had the same enemies and HJM was soon running guns for Mata'afa. When Robert Louis Stevenson arrived a few years later, HJM was one of the first people he met, thanks to a letter of introduction from Fanny's son-in-law. HJM was about the only person in town who had read all his books — and even produced two novels written by himself about his adventures with blackbirders. They enjoyed exchanging stories.

HJM was no pacifist. He told Stevenson of a charge he had led against Tamasese at the head of a band of Mata'afa warriors. He charged across the field on foot, brandishing a sword and waving to his men to follow. At club length from the enemy, he stopped to rally his men, only to find no one behind him. They had disappeared into the woods. With characteristic presence of mind he stopped, smiled, sheathed his sword, and greeted Tamasese as 'the great chief he had come to meet'. His chiefly Samoan speech must have been pretty good because he lived to tell the tale.

Stevenson was enchanted with Moors and accepted HJM's invitation to live with him above the store 'until something better could be arranged.' You can imagine who went ahead to purchase the land, order the materials, supply the groceries, and handle Stevenson's finances — as well as introduce him to Mata'afa. To all three of them politics was endless fascination. Without these contacts Stevenson could never have written *A Footnote to History*. He remained friendly with HJM for the rest of his life. His 'falling out' was only with Fanny. Unfortunately HJM was in one of his entertainer phases and touring America with his dance troupe when Tusitala died. But he returned to find that his friend had left him some personal mementos; his typewriter, a tea trolley and some crockery from the great hall at Vailima, as well as photographs of their good times together. If you want to see them now ask 'Uncle Harry's' children.

But Stevenson's relationship to full Samoans is deeper than politics. It may have something to do with temperament. His outlook on life may have been more congenial to them than to local Europeans. It was more than bare feet and casual clothes — some of his natural impulses were surprisingly Samoan. Great chiefs do not hide their riches. They display them in lavish gestures of hospitality and never spoil the occasion with worries about cost. According to HJM, who did worry about his bills, Tusitala favoured the Samoan rather than the Scotch model. Vailima was the most sumptuous 'maota' (chief's house) in Samoa. It was open to all and the food was unbelievable. Samoans instinctively felt themselves in the presence of the great chief. And there were corroborating signs as well. Chiefs (and their wives) give commands, expect obedience, and reward exceptional service by adoption into the clan. It is quite possible that Tusitala's household staff, Talolo, Sosimo, Iopu, Misifolo and the rest, were moved rather than annoyed when told to change from their own lavalavas to ones of Stuart tartan when serving guests. The cut was congenial but it was the colours that counted. They showed the world that High Chief Tusitala had honoured them with adoption into his own clan. And there is that other half of the chief-tautua relationship as well. The former do not pay well but do come through in a personal way in times of trouble. Fanny may not have been easy to work for, but in the flu epidemic of 1893 she turned the banquet hall into an infirmary and made soup for sick staff — *herself* — sure sign of a true 'faletua' (chief's wife).

Going even deeper are matters of intuitive belief. Save for the Bible, Samoan mothers and grandmothers, do not read to their children. Instead, on moonlit nights in darkened 'fales' (Samoan thatched houses) when 'aitu' (spirits are apt to be abroad, they lie with their youngsters on pandanus mats and tell 'fagogo', stories laced with laughter and song but also unearthly happenings haunting the spine-tingling edges of credibility. 'Fagogo' leave a profound impression and not only on children. They explain strange things that cannot be accounted for in a more rational manner. My mother-in-law was a pastor's wife, but also a great teller of fagogo. One of her favourite stories had particular credibility because it came, of all places, from an old missionary journal 'O le Sulu o Samoa' in unmistakeable missionary Samoan. Missionaries certainly do not print things that are untrue. The story had to do with an 'aitu' caught in a bottle. If its owner rubbed the bottle the 'aitu' would give him anything he wanted except eternal life (since that power was reserved to missionaries). But sooner or later the 'aitu' would kill any owner who did not pass the bottle on. By the time she was telling that story to her own 14 children in the 1920's and 30's it had the ring of a true fagogo. Didn't it explain Vailima? How could

Tusitala, who was neither trader nor governor, come by such a wondrous mansion? The poor man must have been caught with the bottle; that heartless imp killed him. Didn't we bury his body on Mt Vaea? It wasn't until years later, at school in America, that my husband read Stevenson's story of 'The Bottle Imp'. His mother and Tusitala had one gift in common — the ability to tell fagogo so well they half convinced themselves.

Samoans do not need Tusitala to tell them of the female 'aitu' named Saumaiafe who flits around the rainforest at night clad only in her long hair. When caught alone at night among the giant trees, Samoans have felt the sudden chill and rising hair that shows she is nearby. But sometimes it is handy that Tusitala was able to describe those feelings so vividly. I know a young Samoa, with smiling eyes, who left the chapter about Saumaiafe open on the desk of a 'palagi' girl he wanted to meet. Of course she was intrigued and went out to find who had left it there. Now they are married with seven children, fourteen grandchildren and living in Samoa. A writer who can do that is worth remembering.

The future of that lanky Scotchman who dared take our side, spend money like a chief, and share our scariest feelings, is assured immortality as long as the name Tusitala is whispered at night in fagogo to Samoan children.

HIGH CHIEF
MATA'AFA

TO THE STEVENSON
FELLOWSHIP
(SAN FRANCISCO 5 OCTOBER 1904)

MATA'AFA'S ADDRESS

Blows the wind to-day, and the sun and the rain are
  flying,
Blows the wind on the moors to-day and now,
Where about the graves of the martyrs the whaups are
  crying,
My heart remembers how!
Grey recumbent tombs of the dead in desert places,
Standing stones in the wine-red moor,
Hills of sheep, and the howes of the silent races,
And winds, austere and pure:
Be it granted me to behold you again in dying,
Hills of home! and to hear again the call:
Hear about the graves of the martyrs the peewees crying.
And hear no more at all.

SONGS OF TRAVEL TO

S.R.CROCKETT (VAILIMA)

I, like yourselves, revere the memory of Tusitala. Though the strong hand of death has removed him from our midst, yet the remembrance of his many humane acts, let alone his literary career, will never be forgotten. That household name, Tusitala, is an euphonious to our Samoan ears as much as the name Stevenson is pleasing to all other European friends and admirers. Tusitala was born a hero, and he died a hero among men. He was a man of his word, and a man of deeds, not just words. When I first saw Tusitala, he addressed me and said:

'Samoa is a beautiful country. I like its people and clime, and shall write in my books accordingly. The Samoan Chiefs may be compared to our Scotch Chiefs at home, in regard to their clans.'

'Then stay here with me,' I said, 'and make Samoa your home altogether'.

'That I will, and even if the Lord calls me,' was the reply.

Tusitala-story-writer-spoke the truth, for even now he is still with me in Samoa. Truth is great and must endure. Tusitala's religion and motto was, 'Do ye to others as ye would have them do unto you.' Hence this noble, illustrious man has won my love and admiration, as well as the esteem and respect of all who knew him. My God is the same God who called away Tusitala, and when it has pleased Him for my appointment time to come, then I will gladly join Tusitala in the eternal home where we meet to part no more.

(translation)

LLOYD OSBOURNE

AN INTIMATE
PORTRAIT OF RLS

STEVENSON AT FORTY-THREE

The photographs of Vailima show a large and rather gaunt, barnlike house, disappointingly lacking in picturesqueness. But the photographs, omitting nearly everything save the house, and often taken before the second half was added, convey a very false impression. Not only was it far more attractive than it looks, but it should be visualized in relation to its site, which was superb.

In front, sparkling above the leafy tree-tops, was the vast horizon of the sea; behind was the primeval forest; on one side, rising almost as sheerly as a wall, and densely wooded to its peak, was Mount Vaea; on the other the blue mountains of Atua in the distance. Not another house was visible; not a sign of cultivation except our own; Vailima seemed to stand alone on the island.

Directly in front of the house was a lawn, marked for two tennis-courts, and separated from the green paddock beyond by a long dry-stone wall, which stretched in either direction for about a quarter of a mile. Both in this paddock, and on the land about the house were — here and there — magnificent trees, a hundred and fifty feet in height, which had been spared in clearing away the original forest, and so enormously buttressed at the base that they were eight or ten yards in circumference. A stream on one side of the clearing splashed musically in a series of cascades and ended — as far as we were concerned — in a glorious pool, as clear as crystal, in which we bathed.

There were mango-trees, glossy-leafed breadfruits, lemon-trees, orange-trees, and chiramoyas, with their prickly misshapen fruit, the size of a man's head; avocados, cacao, exquisitely scented *moso'oi* trees, peculiar to Samoa, with their yellow, leaf-like flowers that bloomed thrice a year; pandanus, with their big red seeds that strung with a sweet-smelling wild creeper called *laumaile* were the favourite necklaces of the Samoans; and of course in profusion were cocoanut palms and bananas, which with the breadfruits were in time to supply us with such a large part of our needs. In Vailima there was always a sense of spaciousness; of a big and lordly house set in a park; of wide vistas open to the sea and the breeze. About it all was a rich, glowing, and indescribable natural beauty, which never failed to cause a stranger to exclaim aloud; and being six hundred feet above the sea it had a delightfully fresh climate for so hot a country. The nights were usually cold, especially in the early hours of the morning, and a blanket was essential. Our simple thermometer — a bottle of cocoanut-oil — seldom failed to solidify nightly, which implied fifty-six degrees Fahrenheit.

Within the house the visitor's astonishment grew. Not only

was the main hall extremely large, where a hundred people could dance with ease — but as RLS had imported all his Bournemouth furniture, and much from his father's big house in Edinburgh, one might have thought oneself in civilization, and not thousands of miles away on a remote island of the South Pacific. Pictures, napery, silver — all were in keeping; and except for the rack of rifles and the half-naked servants the illusion was complete; and to realise it to the full it must be remembered that all the other white people, even the highest officials, lived in a rather makeshift way, with the odds and ends they had picked up at auction, and very comfortlessly. Every official term ended in an auction; often I would mark some attractive glasses or coffee-cups, or whatever it was, and say to myself: 'I must buy those in when they are sold.'

In contrast, the dignity, solidity, and air of permanence of Vailima was impressive. It dominated the country like a castle. Chiefs came from the farthest parts of Samoa just to gaze at it and to be led in a hushed and awe-stricken tour of its wonders. When a Samoan said, 'Like the house of Tusitala,' he had reached the superlative. And in this setting, and soon familiar with the language, Stevenson gradually grew into a great feudal chieftain whose word carried weight in a great part of Samoa.

Stevenson made a very large income, and spent it all on Vailima. His letters often show much anxiety about money, and some of his intimate correspondents lectured him severely on his extravagance. Often he lectured himself, often in moments of depression he called Vailima his Abbotsford, and said he was ruining himself like Scott. But his concern ought not to be taken too seriously. Much of the money spent on Vailima was in the nature of capital investment, and once completed — had he never written another line — he could have lived there comfortably, and in no lessened state, on his income from royalties. Moreover, at his mother's death he was to come into a very considerable inheritance from his father. While Vailima was undoubtedly a fantastic extravagance, it was at least within his means, and he had nothing really to fear from the future had he lived.

In recent years people have surprised me by asking, usually in a lowered voice: 'Wasn't Stevenson very morose? Did he not have violent outbreaks of temper, when it was unendurable to live with him? Was that life in Vailima as idyllic as it has been represented to us?'

Like all slanders, there is a germ of truth in this. There were times when Stevenson was terribly on edge with nerves; when he would fly into a passion over nothing; when jaded and weary he would give way to fits of irritability that were hard indeed to bear. But it must be remembered that he was one of the most unselfish, lofty-minded, and generous of men; there was no pettiness in him — nothing ignoble or mean. He was no petulant sick man raging at his family because one of his comforts had been overlooked. Rather was it the other way. He cared nothing for risk or danger, and went into it with an appalling unconcern. Of all things he hated most were anxious efforts to guard his health or make him comfortable. Once I tried to put a mattress on the bare boards he slept on. It was like disturbing a tiger! The mattress almost went out the window. Such passions were not without their humor, and afterward Stevenson was often as ready to laugh over them as we.

The sad part of life in Vailima was of that great, striving heart in so frail a body; the sight of that wistful face, watching us at tennis, which after but a single game, had ended — for him — in a haemorrhage; the anguish which underlay that invincible optimism, and which at rare moments would become tragically apparent; the sense of a terrible and unequal struggle; the ineffable pity swelling in one's breast until it became almost insupportable.

That was the shadow on Vailima.

It was usually a very jolly party that sat round the big table; laughter abounded, and Stevenson in general was in excellent spirits. It was a point of honor with any of us going down to Apia to bring back a budget of news, and the merrier the better. And the little town, to anyone with a sense of humor, brimmed over with the ridiculous.

That Stevenson sometimes chafed against his enforced exile is only too true. There are passages in his letters that read very pathetically. But had his health improved, and had he returned to Europe, would he really have been content in some more pretentious 'Skerryvore' or 'La Solitude'? I cannot think so.

His life of feudal splendor in Samoa would have seemed twice as resplendent in the retrospect, and in some French or Italian villa I believe he would have broken his heart to return. Samoa filled his need for the dramatic and the grandiose; he expanded on its teeming stage, where he could hold warriors in leash and play Richelieu to half-naked kings. He had been touched by that most consuming of all ambitions — stagecraft — and there was in him, hardly realized but emerging, the spirit of a great administrator, slowly bringing order out of chaos and finding immeasurable joy in the task.

Sir George Grey, one of the greatest of English pro-consuls, appreciated this, when he said so earnestly at parting with Stevenson: 'Go back; fight on, and never lose heart — for your place is in Samoa, and you must never think of leaving it.'

Stevenson may not have been always happy in Vailima, but of one thing I am sure; he was happier there than he could have been in any place in the world.

THE DEATH OF STEVENSON

Stevenson had never appeared so well as during the months preceding his death, and there was about him a strange serenity which it is hard to describe, for in quoting from his talks I might easily convey a sense of depression and disillusionment that would read like a contradiction. I think he must have had some premonition of his end; at least he spoke often of his past as though he were reviewing it, and with a curious detachment as though it no longer greatly concerned him.

'I am the last of Scotland's three Robbies,' he said once. *'Robbie Burns, Robbie Fergusson, and Robbie Stevenson — and how hardly life treated them all, poor devils! If ever I go back I shall put up a stone to poor Fergusson on that forgotten grave of his.'*

Then he repeated the words in broad Scots as though their cadence pleased him: 'Scotland's three Robbies!'

On another occasion he said to me: 'I am not a man of any unusual talent, Lloyd; I started out with very modest abilities; my success has been due to my really remarkable industry — to developing what I had in me to the extreme limit. When a man begins to sharpen one faculty, and keeps on sharpening it with tireless perseverance, he can achieve wonders. Everybody knows it; it's a commonplace, and yet how rare it is to find anybody doing it — I mean to the uttermost as I did. What genius I had was for work!'

Another observation of his comes back to me: 'A writer who amounts to anything is constantly dying and being reborn. I was reading 'Virginibus' the other day, and it seemed to me extraordinarily good, but in a vein I could no more do now than I could fly. My work is profounder than it was; I can touch emotions that I then scarcely knew existed; but the Stevenson who wrote 'Virginibus' is dead and buried, and has been for many a year.'

'We don't live for the necessities of life; in reality no one cares a damn for them; what we live for are its superfluities.'

'The saddest object in civilization and to my mind the greatest confession of its failure, is the man who can work, who wants to work, and who is not allowed to work.'

Several times he referred to his wish be buried on the peak of Mount Vaea. Although it was on our property and was always conspicuously in our view, Stevenson was the only one of us who had ever scaled its precipitous slopes. But in spite of his request I never could bring myself to cut a path to the summit. I knew it would be a terrific task, but this was not my real objection. I shrank, as may be imagined, from the association with his death that it involved. What was it but the path to his grave? And to work on it was unutterably repugnant to me. Thus in spite of his vexation I always contrived to evade his desire.

In the late afternoons as some of us played tennis in front of the house he would walk up and down the veranda, and I began to notice how often he stopped to gaze up at the peak. It was specially beautiful at dusk with the evening star shining above it, and it was then he would pause the longest in an abstraction that disturbed me. I always tried to interrupt such reveries; would call to him; ask him the score; would often drop out of a game in order to join him and distract his attention. It is a curious thing that his previous illnesses, which might so easily have concluded in his death, caused me less anguish than the look on his face as he now stared up at Vaea. I think it was the realization that he meant to fight no longer; that his unconquerable spirit was breaking; that he was not unwilling to lie on the spot he had chosen and close his eyes forever.

Yet life for us all had never been more pleasant; Samao was enjoying one of its rare spells of peace; the English man-of-war *Curaçoa* had lain so long in port that her officers had become very much our friends, and were constantly staying with us. There were about sixteen of them, and they made a delightful addition to our society; and with several RLS was really intimate. He was working hard on *Weir of Hermiston,* and was more than pleased with his progress. He was well. Why, then, should his glance linger so persistently on the peak of Vaea, and always in that musing way?

It troubled me.

One evening after dinner he read the first chapters of *Weir* aloud. I had my usual pencil and paper for the notes I always took on such occasions, but that night I made none. It was so superbly written that I listened to it in a sort of spell. It seemed absolutely beyond criticism; seemed the very zenith of anything he had ever accomplished, it flowed with such an inevitability and emotion, such a sureness and perfection, that the word seemed to strike against my heart. When he had finished I sat dumb. I knew I should have spoken, but I could not. The others praised it; lauded it to the skies; but I was in a dream from which I could not awake. I poured out a whisky and soda for myself, and sat there like a clod, looking at the ceiling.

Then the party broke up, and we dispersed on our different ways to bed; I out of doors, to go to my own cottage a few hundred yards away. I had hardly passed the threshold of the door, however when I heard Stevenson behind me. He was in a state of frightful agitation; was trembling, breathless, almost beside himself. 'My God, you shall not go like that!' he cried out, seizing me by the arm, and his thin fingers closing on it like a vice. 'What! Not a single note, not a single word, not even the courtesy of a lie! You, the only one whose opinion I depend on, and all you can say is: 'Good night, Louis!' So that is your decision, is it? Just 'Good night, Louis,' — like a blow in the face!'

The bitterness and passion he put into these words are

beyond any power of mine to describe.

Then he went on in the same appalling key of reproach while I listened like the criminal I felt I was. Never had he been so humiliated; never had he been so intolerably insulted. He was no child who had always to have his lollipops; he could brace himself for any criticism, no matter how damning. But the contempt of silence! That sitting there and saying nothing! The implication that it was too bad even to discuss. All that preparation to take notes, and then not a damned word! Unworthy even of notes, was it? Good God, it was more than he could bear!

Put yourself in my place; try to imagine my feelings; I who had been so carried away by *Weir* that this was the ironical climax! Oh, that idiotic silence! What had possessed me? I had known all the while it was inexcusable, yet I had sat there looking at the ceiling, oblivious of the author and thinking only of the book.

Then I tried to tell him the truth, but with difficulty, realizing how unpardonably I had hurt his pride, which was really more concerned than the question of my judgement. That it was a masterpiece; that never before had he written anything comparable with *Weir;* that it promised to be the greatest novel in the English language.

We were in the dark. I could not see his face. But I believe he listened with stupefaction. The reaction when it came was too great for his sorely strained nerves; tears rained from his eyes, and mine too, streamed. Never had I known him to be so moved; never had I been so moved myself; and in the all-pervading darkness we were for once free to be ourselves, unashamed. Thus we sat, with our arms about each other, talking far into the night. Even after thirty years I should not care to divulge anything so sacred as those confidences; the revelation of that tortured soul; the falterings of its Calvary. Until then I had never conceived the degree of his daily suffering; the petty, miserable dragging ailments that kept him in a 'perpetual torment.' He spoke of the 'physical dishonor'; of the 'degradation' of it; of moments when he had longed for death. To me his heroism took on new proportions, and I was thankful I had refused an important post in order to stay with him. 'It will not be for long,' he said.

At parting he told me to remind him of this talk if we should ever have the slightest misunderstanding again; but while such was its meaning, no words can convey the tenderness of its expression — the softened voice, the eyes suffusing in the starlight, the lingering clasp of the hand. That night of *Weir* evokes the most affecting of all my recollections.

HMS *Curaçao*, with all those good friends on board, left us in November; and the weather, as though in mourning, broke in deluges of rain. The wet season, as it is called, begins in November, and with it a heat and stickiness, an oppressiveness, lifelessness, and debilitation that make this period of the year something to dread. But we were fortunate in having a pleasant intermission for the 13th — RLS's birthday — when we gave a great Samoan party, which, including the retainers and hangers-on — are an inseparable part of such an entertainment — brought up over a hundred people. Then the rain poured again, and kept pouring until the beginning of December, when there was another sunny interval. After dinner on the evening of the 2nd, RLS, who was in excellent spirits, surprised us by proposing we should play some games.

'We are getting horribly dull up here,' he said. 'Everybody sticks round a lamp with a book, and it is about as gay as a Presbyterian mission for seamen. Let's play a game I have just thought of.'

The game consisted of each in turn entering the room and in pantomime, with any accessories we could lay our hands on portraying one of our friends or acquaintances for the others to guess at. We started a little self-consciously; none but RLS was very eager about it; but in a short time we were wildly hilarious and continued the pastime with shouts of laughter. RLS excelled everyone; there was a touch of Lauder in his broad, rich characterizations and in the exuberance of his own pleasure in them. We kept at it long after our usual bedtime, and our good-nights were said amid giggles of recollection. It was one of the most amusing evenings we had ever spent in Vailima — and was Stevenson's last.

The next day I had some business in Apia, and did not return until late in the afternoon. The weather had been so good that

I left word to have one of the tennis-courts mown and re-marked; but as we no longer needed two, since the *Curaçao* had gone, I had told my men to ignore the second except to cut the grass. I regretted my decision when I saw what they had done, which had been to inscribe, L O I A, in gigantic white letters, covering the entire court! It had the silliest look. What a spectacle for any supercilious officials paying a formal call! But there it was, flattering and absurd, and supposed to be a pleasant surprise for me!

RLS was dictating some of *Weir* to my sister, and they both seemed glad to stop and listen to the budget of news I had brought up. But first I led them to the window and showed them the lawn, the sight of which — and to my annoyance — sent them off into peals of laughter. Then after a little talk, which looking back on it, I recall as even gayer than usual, I went over to the cottage to change and have a plunge in the pool. I was away perhaps an hour or more — when I heard a curious stir in the house and a voice calling my name. Tragedy always has its note. The intonation was sufficient to send me in startled haste across the way.

Stevenson was lying back in an armchair, unconscious, breathing stertorously and with his unseeing eyes wide open; and on either side of him were my mother and sister, pale and apprehensive. They told me in whispers that he had suddenly cried out: 'My head — oh, my head,' and then had fallen insensible. For a while we fanned him, put brandy to his lips, strove in vain to rouse him by speaking. We could not bring ourselves to believe he was dying. Then we had a cot brought down, and, taking him in my arms — it was pitiable how light he was — I carried him to it and extended him at length. By this time the truth was evident to us; that he had an apoplectic stroke. His reddened face and that terrible breathing were only too conclusive.

I had our fastest horse saddled and brought to the door 'Saumaiafe,' a blood mare that had won several races — and off I went at breakneck speed for the doctor in Apia. I was lucky in finding him — a short, thick-set, rather portly German, with most of his face hidden in gray whiskers and not unlike the portraits of Von Tirpitz. At my urgings — I simply would not tolerate any denial — he timidly mounted my horse, giving me the little black bag he dared not carry himself. With this in my hand I ran after him through the town, hoping to find a tethered horse on the way. Sure enough there was one, and in an instant I was on it and galloping off while its astonished owner, emerging from a bar, gazed after me with amazement. Soon overtaking the doctor, we went on together at a speed miserably disproportionate to the suspense I was in, while he gravely questioned me, and muttered 'Ach, ach!' in none too hopeful a tone.

Stevenson was still breathing in that dreadful way. The doctor looked down at him long and earnestly and then almost imperceptibly shook his head.

'A blood clot on the brain,' he said. 'He is dying.'

In half an hour, at about eight in the evening, Stevenson was dead.

On leaving, the doctor said to me in a low and significant voice: 'You must bury him before three to-morrow.'

Misunderstanding my look of horror, he murmured something more in the way of explanation. But I was thinking of that path to Vaca; that path I had never made; of Stevenson's wish which I had always thwarted. Were he to be buried on the summit that path had to be made between dawn and three o'clock the next day. It seemed impossible, but I said to myself: 'It has to be done! It has to be done!' I had failed the living, but I would not fail the dead. In desperation I sent out messengers to several of my closest friends — chiefs whom I relied on like brothers. I needed two hundred men at dawn and explained the urgency. But the axes, the bush knives, the mattocks, picks, spades, and crowbars? Vailima had no more than sufficient for thirty, and I doubted if the chiefs could equip as many more. In bitter perplexity I went back to consult my mother, who reminded me we should also need some kind of mourning for these men.

By this time the news of RLS's death had spread far and wide, and Samoan messengers were beginning to arrive from every direction, facilitating our task. The upshot of it was that we had one of the shops opened in the town and arrangements made to bring up the necessary tools, as well as hundreds of white singlets and dozens of bolts of black cotton cloth. Two yards of this wide, black cotton would suffice to make a *lavalava*, as the kilt-like Samoan garment is called; and in these and white-cotton undershirts our Vailima retainers would make a creditable appearance, and one which they would consider appropriate.

Mr Clarke, one of our missionary friends, arrived to volunteer his invaluable services, and to him was confided the duty of finding a coffin and having it sent up at dawn; he was also given a list of those who were to be specially invited for the funeral next day at two o'clock. The suddenness of this planning was almost overwhelming; we were half distracted by it; the only serene and untroubled face was that of Tusitala, lying there at peace.

Late that night we washed his body and dressed it in a soft white-linen shirt and black evening trousers girded with a dark-blue silk sash. A white tie, dark-blue silk socks, and patent leather shoes completed the costume. The sash may sound extraordinary, but it was the custom to wear sashes in Samoa. Indeed, the whole costume seems to call for some explanation. Except for the short white mess jacket, which was omitted, it was our usual evening dress; though it is impossible to recollect why this was chosen in preference to the white clothes ordinarily worn in the daytime. Possibly it was decided by those patent-leather shoes, which RLS had always liked so much, and which showed off his slender and shapely feet to such perfection.

Stevenson had never cared for jewellery of any kind; except for his studs and sleeve-links he had nothing but a plain silver ring, which we left on his finger. This was the ring with which he had plighted his troth with my mother so many years before and similar to the one she always wore herself; perhaps they had not been able to afford gold in those early days, or may have preferred the homely peasant silver from some association connected with it. I gazed at it with moistened eyes, this symbol of bygone romance which had come so far to lie at last on Vaea.

Placing the body on our big table, we drew over it the red English ensign, twelve feet long and proportionately broad, that we habitually flew over the house. Then candles were lighted, and a little part of our Samoans, begging us to retire, took on themselves the self-appointed duty of spending the night beside the bier. They were all Roman Catholics, and at intervals intoned Latin prayers in unison. There was a wonderful beauty in the cadence of that old, old tongue, so sonorous, so impressive, and so strange to hear on such lips. All that night as I tried to sleep the murmur of it was in my ears.

Before dawn Vailima began to seethe with men, one little army after another marching up with its chiefs. I went out and greeted them, and then we had a little council together — these tall, grave men so understanding and so used to command, who quietly apportioned the work between themselves and lost no time in fruitless discussion. Tusitala's wish would be obeyed; it was as sacred to them as it was to me. In turn, they volunteered their assurance that by two o'clock the path would be ready and the grave dug on the summit of Vaea.

All that morning the still air was broken by the crash of trees; the ringing sound of axes, the hoarser thud of mattocks and crowbars, pounding on rocks. But the men themselves had been warned to make no sound; there was none of the singing and laughter that was such an inseparable part of concerted work. Silent, glistening with sweat and in a fury of effort, each strove with axe or bush knife, with mattock, spade or pick to pay his last tribute to Tusitala. I made my way through them to the summit, and chose the spot for the grave. The view from it was incomparable; the rim of the sea, risen to the height of one's eyes, gave a sense of infinite vastness; and it was all so lonely, so wild, so incredibly beautiful, that one stood there awestricken.

All that morning Stevenson's body lay in state, and in succession chief after chief arrived to pay his last homage. Each carried an *ie longa,* one of those priceless old mats so finely woven that they are as soft and pliable as a piece of silk, and which are valued in the degree of their antiquity. With an *ie longa* in his hand each chief advanced alone, and, stopping within a dozen feet of the body, addressed it as though it were alive. It was a touching rite, and some of the speeches were exceedingly eloquent. One old chief, whom I had never seen before and whose harsh features and sullen expression impressed me at first very unfavourably, brought the finest mat of all, and made a speech that moved everyone to tears. He had a voice of magnificent range, the diction of a most accomplished orator, a power of pathos I have never heard equalled.

'Samoa end with you, Tusitala,' he concluded in a peroration of tragic intensity. 'When death closed the eyes of our best and greatest friend, we knew as a race that our own day was done.'

An unexampled number of fine mats were brought and laid on Stevenson's body, so many that the flag was entirely heaped with them; and amongst them some so ancient that they were almost black and needed care in handling them. Samoans have nothing more precious. *Ie longa* represent jewellery, riches, social position; some specially famous have individual names; some in conferring exalted rank are an inseparable part of native nobility; murders have been committed for them; families squabble furiously over their disposition, beginning feuds that last for generations. Yet the irony is that they are of no practical worth whatever, and are never so coveted as when almost falling to pieces with age. Ours we returned afterward to all the various donors. Knowing their value, we had not the heart to retain them when we left Samoa.

At two o'clock the coffin was brought out by a dozen powerful Samoans, who led the way with it up the mountain. Directly behind were thirty or forty more men, who at intervals changed places with the bearers. It was a point of honour with them all to keep their heavy burden shoulder-high, though how they contrived to do so on that precipitous path was a seeming impossibility. A party of a score or more white people followed, interspersed with chiefs of high rank. Behind these, again, were perhaps two hundred Samoans, all in the white singlets and black *lavalavas* which had been given them for that day of mourning.

The sun shone mercilessly; the heat was stifling; but of course our own feeling was one of thankfulness that rain had not intervened. A heavy rain in Samoa is a veritable cloudburst. We should never have been able to make the path had it rained, and the whole interment would have been robbed of its dignity and beauty. But the heat made it a terrible climb for some of our guests. There was one elderly white man who I thought

would never reach the summit alive. We knew him but slightly;
were surprised, indeed, to see him; I doubt if Stevenson had
ever spoken to him more than half a dozen times.

'I am going on if it kills me,' he said, deaf to all our entreaties
to turn back. 'I venerated Stevenson; he shall not be laid in his
grave without my last tribute of respect.'

With mottled face, shirt half open, gasping for breath and
occasionally lying down while we fanned him he persevered
with an almost irritating obstinacy. But I really did believe it did
kill him, for the poor fellow was ill for a month afterward and
then died. There were others who looked almost as spent, but
who were animated by a similar resolution. The photographs
of Mount Vaea, like all photographs of mountains, diminish its
height; it would be easy for one who has seen it only in pictures
to get a very mistaken impression. From Vailima to the summit
is a most formidable ascent for sedentary people unaccustomed
to exercise.

We gathered about the grave, and no cathedral could have
seemed nobler or more hallowed than the grandeur of nature
that encompassed us. What fabric of men's hands could vie
with so sublime a solitude? The sea in front, the primeval forest
behind, crags, precipices, and distant cataracts gleaming in an
untrodden wilderness. The words of the Church of England
service, movingly delivered, broke the silence in which we
stood. The coffin was lowered; flowers were strewn on it, and
then the hurrying spades began to throw back the earth.

"Under the wide and starry sky,
Dig the grave and let me lie.
Glad did I live and gladly die,
And I laid me down with a will.

This be the verse you grave for me:
Here he lies where he longed to be,
Home is the sailor, home from sea,
And the hunter home from the hill."

LAST WORD

(Written on top of Mount Vaea, Apia, Western Samoa. Channelled by E.S.W. — approx. 1.15pm, 3.3.1991)

It is the power of words that will link with love and feelings. Words speak, words tell, words link mankind with their higher being. Words destroy confidence and the power of words never fail, so use them carefully; use them well and always with love and lightness. Be open and soft and gentle with them, being light as a feather. Always to hear and be aware of the Samoan people. My heart is close at hand; to be near and make life richer and clearer. But be careful not to change, to lose the gentle heart and self, that is their own. Too often the spoken word works against their kindly ways. So be at all times aware of gentle customs and speak to the gentle, soft side with thoughts and listen, listen, listen for it is in listening comes awareness of the next step. Be conscious of those that speak the quiet language, not just the brassy noises. The ones that demand to be heard are not the ones to listen to. It must be about words, not things. I cared not one whit for things. They were an encumbrance to my life. I cared for words, they were my stock and trade. My life always when ill (and gone in other ways) were the words. They danced in my head and kept me company. When I could not talk they were my friends, my company of angels about me, my words always at my beck and call. I could not always capture their essence and they eluded me and danced away, coy things to be run after, coy creatures, my friends the words. So make this a memorial to my friends the words. I want them heard, all about. The Samoans knew how to capture the spirit essence of these friends the words and they knew we each, in our own language, had these same spirits about us. Let this enterprise give homage to their word spirits not worldly goods. They are only man's servants not man's gods. So let them go and make it so all those that want to write can find comfort in the person who made this friendship and understood its importance. If you tell the Samoan people it is to be a temple to the spirit of words and not material things then they will understand.

All should come together, writers of all nations to learn from these simple folk the beauty about them and the Samoan lesson will be heard far and wide. The people gather for the concerts and festivals of music, so will they gather at the place Vailima for a festival of words and speak from the heart. Not of the material but of the spiritual. That is why you are all brought together because you can see this end but it can go otherwise if you are not careful and it must not be about power or the powerful. Keep it at all times simple. When it becomes complex then stop. Examine. There is something wrong. Go back always to the simple. I often made this mistake on earth and it cost me dear in time and effort and I had a hard lesson to learn. I wished for more simple life and got caught in complexities. Do not, repeat not, make the same mistake. Stop and listen and you will hear in quiet time. Yes, it will come to pass. You are good and understand the Samoans themselves. Understand but beware of the part in all men that goes beyond the simple truth of it. Examine and be aware. Love and happiness, dear, funny, tired person. Thought you could not make it? You will come. Many more times up the mountain. It is a beautiful place of tranquility. It must never change. Life is a long hard trek, out of breath, heart pumping but keep working upward, upward. The rewards are great at the end. The peace and light and air and light of the being is at the end and when the final steps are made then the final reward is peace but there must be effort given along the way. That is man's test, that he keep tramping higher and higher. Lest he fail to recognize what he is after, there are the words, the spirit of the words to give him aid.

CHRONOLOGY

1850 13 November, born Edinburgh.

1857 Began education at Henderson's Preparatory School, Edinburgh.

1867 Stevenson enters Edinburgh University, to study engineering.

1871 April: gives up engineering for law; Autumn: begins legal training with WF Skene & Peacock.

1872 July: visits Germany.

1873 First published essay: 'Roads'.

1874 April: in Menton, France; May—June: in Scotland; June: London, elected to Savile Club; Summer: cruises Inner Hebrides; December, London and Cambridge.

1875 Spring: visits artists' colonies in France. July: called to the Scottish Bar.

1876 January: walking tour in Ayrshire and Galloway. Summer: he meets Fanny Osbourne at Grèz-sur-Loing, France, and remains in France during Autumn.

1877 Much of the year in Paris with Fanny Osbourne. First published short story: 'A Lodging for the Night'.

1878 First book published: *An Inland Voyage*. Autumn: walking tour of Cévennes. *Cévennes Journal*; and *Edinburgh: Picturesque Notes* published. Winter in London and Scotland.

1879 January in Scotland, at work on *Deacon Brodie* with Henley. *Travels with a Donkey in the Cévennes* published. August, sails for New York; Autumn: in Monterey, California.

1880 May: marries Fanny Osbourne in San Francisco; honeymoon at Silverado, Napa County. August, returns to Edinburgh with Fanny and stepson Lloyd Osbourne. Winter in Davos, Switzerland.

1881 *Virginibus Puerisque* published. May: in France; June—September in Scotland, beginning *Treasure Island* at Braemar; winter in Switzerland.

1882 *Familiar Studies of Men and Books*, and *New Arabian Nights* published. Summer in Scotland. October: moves to St Marcel, near Marseilles, France.

1883 *Treasure Island* published. Living in France most of the year.

1884 *The Silverado Squatters* published. January—July living in France, returns to London in the summer, on to Wensleydale and Bournemouth.

1885 Settled in Bournemouth. Published: *A Child's Garden of Verses; More New Arabian Nights (The Dynamiter)*, and *Prince Otto*.

1886 *Dr Jekyll and Mr Hyde*, and *Kidnapped* published.

1887 May: to Scotland on father's death. August: sails for New York, September at Newport, settles at Saranac Lake. *Memories and Portraits; The Merry Men and Other Tales,* and *Memoir of Fleeming Jenkin* (biography); *Underwoods* (poems), published.

1888 *The Black Arrow* published. April: in New York; May: in New Jersey. South Seas voyage: to the Marquesas, the Paumotus, the Society Islands, by December: the Sandwich Islands, and Honolulu.

1889 Published: *The Wrong Box* (with Lloyd Osbourne), and *The Master of Ballantrae*. June: sets out for the Gilbert Islands; December: first sight of Samoa, and he purchases land to build Vailima.

1890 February: Sydney, Australia. April—August, cruise to the Gilbert, Marshall and other islands, and New Caledonia; August-September: Sydney. October: settles in Samoa; November: building of Vailima. *In The South Seas*; and *Ballads* (poems), published.

1891 His mother arrives in Sydney from Scotland, escorts her to Samoa.

1892 Published: *Across the Plains; A Footnote to History;* and *The Wrecker* (with Lloyd Osbourne);and *Beau Austin; Deacon Brodie; Admiral Guinea* (plays with Henley).

1893 Published: *Island Nights' Entertainment;* and *Catriona*. Vailima is complete. February: in Sydney. August: outbreak of civil war in Samoa, defeat of Chief Mataafa. September—October: Honolulu.

1894 Abandons writing *St Ives* for *Weir of Hermiston*. *The Ebb Tide* (with Lloyd Osbourne) published. Samoan chiefs build road in gratitude to him, with feast on his 44th birthday.

3 December: Vailima, Stevenson dies of cerebral haemorrage.

1895 Published: *The Amateur Emigrant; Macaire* (play with Henley)

1896 Published: *St Ives; Weir of Hermiston; Songs of Travel* (poems); *Records of a Family of Engineers* (biography).

1898 Published: *The Charity Bazaar* (play); *Moral Emblems* (poems).

1922 *The Hanging Judge* (play with Mrs R L Stevenson)

1924 *New Poems*

1928 *Monmouth: A Tragedy* (incomplete play with R Stevenson).

1956 *Our Samoan Adventure* (with Mrs R L Stevenson).